POSTILS for PREACHING

POSTILS for PREACHING
Commentaries on the Revised Common Lectionary, Year B

John Rollefson

RESOURCE *Publications* • Eugene, Oregon

POSTILS FOR PREACHING
Commentaries on the Revised Common Lectionary, Year B

Copyright © 2016 John Rollefson. All rights reserved. Except for brief quotations in critical publications or reviews, no part of this book may be reproduced in any manner without prior written permission from the publisher. Write: Permissions, Wipf and Stock Publishers, 199 W. 8th Ave., Suite 3, Eugene, OR 97401.

Resource Publications
An Imprint of Wipf and Stock Publishers
199 W. 8th Ave., Suite 3
Eugene, OR 97401

www.wipfandstock.com

PAPERBACK ISBN: 978-1-4982-9049-4
HARDCOVER ISBN: 978-1-4982-9051-7
EBOOK ISBN: 978-1-4982-9050-0

Manufactured in the U.S.A.

Scripture quotations are from the New Revised Standard Version of the Bible, copyright 1989 National Council of the Churches of Christ in the USA.

To Ruth, my comrade in (loving) arms
and to the congregations that gracefully and (usually)
gratefully received the Word.

And to Mary who graciously came to my rescue.

And he (Jesus) said to them: "Therefore every scribe who has been trained for the kingdom of heaven is like the master of a household who brings out of his treasure what is new and what is old."

—Matt 13:52

Contents

Preface | xi

SEASON OF ADVENT | 3
   First Sunday of Advent | 3
   Second Sunday of Advent | 5
   Third Sunday of Advent | 8
   Fourth Sunday of Advent | 10

SEASON OF CHRISTMAS | 14
   Nativity of Our Lord, Christmas Eve | 14
   Nativity of Our Lord, Christmas Day | 14
   First Sunday of Christmas | 14
   Second Sunday of Christmas | 17
   Epiphany of Our Lord | 17

TIME AFTER EPIPHANY | 18
   Baptism of Our Lord, First Sunday
      after Epiphany, Lectionary 1 | 18
   Second Sunday after Epiphany, Lectionary 2 | 22
   Third Sunday after Epiphany, Lectionary 3 | 25
   Fourth Sunday after Epiphany, Lectionary 4 | 29
   Fifth Sunday after Epiphany, Lectionary 5 | 32
   Sixth Sunday after Epiphany, Lectionary 6 | 35
   Seventh Sunday after Epiphany, Lectionary 7 | 39
   Eighth Sunday after Epiphany, Lectionary 8 | 42
   Transfiguration of Our Lord, Last Sunday after Epiphany | 44

SEASON OF LENT | 48

Ash Wednesday | 48
First Sunday in Lent | 48
Second Sunday in Lent | 51
Third Sunday in Lent | 54
Fourth Sunday in Lent | 57
Fifth Sunday in Lent | 60

HOLY WEEK | 63

Sunday of the Passion/Palm Sunday | 63
Maundy Thursday | 65
Good Friday | 65
Vigil of Easter | 65
Resurrection of Our Lord, Easter Day | 65
Second Sunday of Easter | 68
Third Sunday of Easter | 71
Fourth Sunday of Easter | 73
Fifth Sunday of Easter | 76
Sixth Sunday of Easter | 78
Ascension of Our Lord | 81
Seventh Sunday of Easter | 81
The Day of Pentecost | 84

TIME AFTER PENTECOST, YEAR B | 87

Holy Trinity Sunday, First Sunday after Pentecost | 87
Lectionary 8, Proper 3 | 90
Lectionary 9, Proper 4 | 90
Lectionary 10, Proper 5 | 93
Lectionary 11, Proper 6 | 96
Lectionary 12, Proper 7 | 99
Lectionary 13, Proper 8 | 101
Lectionary 14, Proper 9 | 105
Lectionary 15, Proper 10 | 107
Lectionary 16, Proper 11 | 110
Lectionary 17, Proper 12 | 113
Lectionary 18, Proper 13 | 115
Lectionary 19, Proper 14 | 118
Lectionary 20, Proper 15 | 120
Lectionary 21, Proper 16 | 123

Lectionary 22, Proper 17 | 126
Lectionary 23, Proper 18 | 129
Lectionary 24, Proper 19 | 132
Lectionary 25, Proper 20 | 135
Lectionary 26, Proper 21 | 138
Lectionary 27, Proper 22 | 141
Lectionary 28, Proper 23 | 144
Lectionary 29, Proper 24 | 147
Lectionary 30, Proper 25 | 150
Reformation Sunday | 153
All Saints Day | 153
Lectionary 31, Proper 26 | 155
Lectionary 32, Proper 27 | 158
Lectionary 33, Proper 28 | 162
Christ the King, (Reign of Christ),
    Lectionary 34, Proper 29 | 164
Day of Thanksgiving | 167

Bibliography | 171

Preface

What's A Postil?

My *Oxford English Dictionary* (in the compact edition which can only be read through a magnifying glass) defines "postil" as "a marginal note or comment upon a text of scripture" or "a series of such comments, a commentary or exposition; especially an expository discourse or homily upon the Gospel or Epistle for the day read or intended to be read in the church service."[1] This antique word of "uncertain origin" might derive from the Latin words *"post illa"* meaning "after those" (words of the text) that they were meant to illumine. At any rate it's an obscure word that nicely fits my intention for these "preaching helps" that I offer from my forty years of pastoral experience in reflecting on the appointed texts of scripture that week-in-and-week-out confronted me with the challenge of addressing the living Word to those gathered in worship. While preachers, of course, must be as sensitive to their congregations' contextual complexities as they are responsible to the texts' richness and diversity, for these postils I've tried to make my contextual comments generalized rather than specific, local and dated, suggesting concerns that those who serve as preachers will need to flesh out within their own local situations.

I still remember from early in my ministry an older priest describing his sermon preparation as depending upon a kind of "field-testing" process in which he would consciously take the assigned Word out into the daily rounds of his pastoral ministry. He would employ the texts for the coming Sunday as an interpretive lens through which to see and savor the everyday world into which his calling led him. I've followed my old colleague's advice, often using the appointed psalmody at hospital bedsides, the Gospel

---

1. *Compact Edition of the Oxford English Dictionary*, Vol. II, 2252.

Preface

reading for committee meditations, an Old Testament story at a gathering of children, and the Epistle as a word of blessing or response to the request, "Can you say a little prayer, Pastor?" I once used a passage from Acts 4 from the coming Sunday's lectionary at a meeting of the Los Angeles County Board of Supervisors where I had been asked to "do" the invocation.[2] Such anticipatory field-testing of the assigned texts helped me to root my preaching in the everyday life of my congregation and community and bridge the gap between pulpit and people, between Sunday and Monday.

What follows are not themselves sermons but include exegesis, ideas, illustrations, experiences, connections and references to helpful resources that I have used over the years and have found to further my understanding of the assigned texts and to be especially useful in preparing for speaking the Word for the coming Sunday or other special occasions. My intent in my own preaching is not educational *per se*, to "elevate" or "enlighten" those to whom I intend to speak. It is, rather, "evangelical," in the original meaning of the word, to speak God's good news to the gathered congregation—which never, of course, precludes my own need to hear the gospel. But at the same time, as Luther's preaching makes so clear,[3] sharing knowledge and fresh insights and even explaining difficult words and ideas is not alien to the preacher's calling. Never should one be found "preaching down" to one's congregation from some loftier position either of status or supposed knowledge or experience. But this is no excuse for the "lowlier than thou" attitude Luther detected in his one-time colleague Andreas von Karlstadt and other "enthusiasts" who, Luther feared, didn't adequately respect the Word in their zeal to be one with their congregants.

Care for the words one uses in preaching the Word is a high priority. Lowest-common denominator speech might communicate but often is not sufficiently "roomy," that is, flexible and evocative enough, to embody the richness and depth of the Word. At the same time, I've tried to keep my use of language colloquial and not overly formal, neither fussy nor folksy. I take seriously Jesus' own encouragement in Matthew's Gospel which I've chosen as the epigraph for this book: "*Every scribe who has been trained for the kingdom of heaven is like the master of a household who brings out of his treasure what is new and what is old*" (Matt 13:52). These postils represent

---

2. See my article, "Invoking In Public," 12-14, which both describes the experience and raises serious doubts about what such "invoking" might involve.

3. Timothy Wengert, "Introduction," *The 1529 Holy Week and Easter Sermons of Dr. Martin Luther*, 11-27. It is Wengert's work on sermons from Luther's *Postil* that first suggested the use of the term for my title.

Preface

my best effort to share my "bag of tricks," my "*thesaurus*" in Greek, collected over many years of preaching, with you, my readers.

A few words about the format I've chosen to use are in order. My intention is that each of these postils be a free-standing essay of a thousand to twelve hundred words or so that aims to be helpful to those in preparing to preach the assigned texts for the day. With my strong sense of the seasonal character of the lectionary and the inter-textuality of scripture, occasional reference will be made to earlier or later essays that relate to some point of interest. You will also find me referring more than once to favorite resources, biblical and theological, whenever pertinent. While I understand that the psalmody for the day is not considered, strictly speaking, to be one of the official three appointed texts for the day, I strongly affirm the value of including a reading or singing of the psalm as a part of the liturgy of the day and often find the psalm to provide a nice entrée to the particular liturgical occasion. Each essay, therefore, will be prefaced by a snippet of the psalm for the day. My aim isn't to give equal time to each text (including the Gospel reading) but to let one text lead the way with the others chiming in variously. The postil titles I have provided serve as suggested themes by way of sermon titles I have found helpful in attracting and focusing the congregation's attention. In one congregation I served the practice was for the preacher to write a brief paragraph for the beginning of the printed bulletin to alert folks to the theme of the sermon or some aspect of it. This I have found to be a good discipline for me as preacher whether or not the paragraph is used: to be able to state in a couple of sentences what the sermon aims to say.

The sermon does not a worship service make—even a good one. Here too my favored practice has been to create a sermon that is clearly of one with the liturgy for the day, appropriate to the season of the church year, to the rhythms of the secular world, and in tune with the larger events of the day, including civic and cultural life. The liturgy is the "public service" of the congregation—not just the pastor!—and preaching needs always to be seen as a part of the liturgy. In fact, my days in campus ministry where I preached from the communion table were perhaps my most comfortable, a clear sign that Word and sacrament belong together, and that the eucharist itself is a "visible Word" as Luther liked to put it. This goes too for hymnody and other musical and artistic expression that also bear the Word. I'm a zealous advocate for increasing participation in the music of the global church for worship, and herein the reader will find suggestions for hymns

Preface

that I hope will stretch you beyond the familiar oldies-but-goodies, which, of course, will always also have their place in helping "all God's critters" claim "their place in the choir." I have tried to keep footnotes to a minimum but at the same time am eager both to credit and to share the sources for particular theological insights, textual comments, and illustrative stories that the reader can benefit from consulting.

A final word of explanation regarding where and from whom these postils are coming.

I am an ecumenically-minded Lutheran of the ELCA variety, raised in a low-church Norwegian-American farming community in the upper Midwest. I attended Luther College in Decorah, Iowa, as an undergraduate where I majored in history and classics. While there I was active in drama, student government and intramural athletics as well as becoming increasingly grateful to find my God-given faith mature amid a challenging and supportive setting that claimed the identity of being at once a "community of faith and learning." This propelled me into an adventure of life-long learning that sent me, in time, from New Haven to Edinburgh, from London to Berkeley, and in later years from Collegeville to Cambridge, Mass. Continuing education has nourished a lasting intellectual curiosity that has served me well as a preacher in both urban and campus communities, in small and large congregations, from San Francisco to Milwaukee to Ann Arbor to Los Angeles, with post-retirement interims in Solvang and London. I have been deeply involved in fostering ecumenical relationships and served as an ELCA representative on the Lutheran Reformed Coordinating Committee that led to full communion between our four denominations as well as a delegate to the Ninth Assembly of the Lutheran World Federation in Hong Kong in 1997. While I write self-consciously from the perspective of my Lutheran theological and denominational background and perspective, my aim is to reach as wide an ecumenical audience as is served by the *Revised Common Lectionary*. My wife, Ruth, a retired public vocal music teacher and church musician, has been my partner in life throughout my entire ministry, and my grown sons, Griff and Jake, fellow travelers as preacher's kids. I currently enjoy retirement in San Luis Obispo on California's central coast, where I'm involved in my local congregation and community while enjoying tennis, golf, concerts, reading, writing, wine-tasting, and occasional preaching.

This is the second of an intended three-volume work on the *Revised Common Lectionary* and I encourage my readers to consult my previously

Preface

published *Year A* for postils on those occasions (Christmas, Ash Wednesday, Reformation Sunday, e.g.) when the same lectionary texts are assigned every year. And, of course, please look for my forthcoming *Year C* as well!

Soli Deo Gloria

All Saints 2016

Year B

SEASON OF ADVENT
First Sunday in Advent

Psalm 80:1–7, 17–19
Isaiah 64:1–9
1 Corinthians 1:3–9
Mark 13:24–37

Stir up your might and come to save us!

—Psalm 80:2b

Keep Awake!

Today's readings continue the strong end-time message of the final three Sundays of Year A (Matthew 25's parables of "The Ten Bridesmaids," "The Talents," and "The Final Judgment"). Eschatology moves into a sharply apocalyptic mood as we enter the season of Advent. Using the language of cataclysm, Isaiah pleads for God to "*tear open the heavens and come down*" (v 1). Then he offers images of a tortured nature (all of which, alas, we Californians are much too familiar with): quaking mountains, brush fires, boiling water, and fierce wind.[1]

Our Gospel text, an excerpt from St. Mark's "little apocalypse," opens with Jesus himself indulging in apocalyptic reverie while "*sitting on the Mount of Olives opposite the temple*" (v 3). Like Isaiah before him, Jesus foresees a time of natural cataclysm when "*the sun will be darkened, and the*

---

1. Gowan, *Eschatology in the OT*, 99–120.

moon will not give its light, and the stars will be falling from heaven, and the powers in the heavens will be shaken" (vv 24–25). One can easily see here the inspiration for W. B. Yeats' poem "The Second Coming" with its fear that "the center cannot hold." These signs will precede the coming of the Son of Man, Jesus' favorite way of referencing himself in Mark, "*with great power and glory*" (v 26) accompanied by clouds and angels.

Yet, immediately, Jesus turns to a gentler, softer, and more everyday image from nature to make his point: "*From the fig tree learn its lesson: as soon as its branch becomes tender and puts forth its leaves, you know that summer is near.*" "So," Jesus says, "*when you see these things taking place, you know that he is near, at the very gates*" (vv 28–29). Then follows Jesus' pronouncement that has bedeviled the church at least since Paul's day in seeming so at odds with the so-called "delay of the parousia:" "*Truly I tell you, this generation will not pass away until all these things have taken place,*" (v 30).[2]

Jesus himself is the best interpreter of his own apocalyptic mood, disavowing all subsequent adventisms that would wrong-headedly delight in setting dates for his return. Jesus could not be clearer as he goes on to warn, "*But about that day or hour no one knows, neither the angels in heaven, nor the Son, but only the Father*" (v 32). Instead of speculating, Jesus makes explicit the implication of the imminence of the end time in a series of redundant imperatives: "*beware,*" "*keep alert,*" and then, twice, "*keep awake.*" To clinch his point, Jesus sketches in briefest outline a parable of how someone going on a journey will command the door-keeper to be "*on the watch*" so that when the master returns "*in the evening, or at midnight, or at cockcrow, or at dawn*"(v 35)—"whenever," as we say—the door-keeper will be at the ready. And so, Jesus concludes, "*what I say to you I say to all: Keep awake*" (v 37). This is Jesus' clear mandate regarding the imminence of the end time, and the season of Advent consequently becomes the time for the church to be reminded of its need to stay awake and to ponder the ethical implications of living in a constant state of readiness "*as you wait for the revealing of our Lord Jesus Christ,*"(v 7) as Paul puts it in our second reading.

Singing the old Lutheran warhorse "Wake, Awake, For Night is Flying," (*ELW* #436), the so-called "King of Chorales," is the wake-up call that

---

[2]. See Witherington's, *Jesus, Paul and the End of the World* 20–22 for a reassessment of Albert Schweitzer's conclusions regarding Jesus as apocalyptic prophet as well as Juel's *Master of Suspense*, 77–80.

Advent is upon us for many Lutherans and others, but also see the equally popular oldie from Charles Wesley, "Lo! He Comes with Clouds Descending" (*ELW* #435).

Some years ago a fellow pastor proposed that the church finally acknowledge defeat and accede to the culture that has been rushing toward Christmas since Halloween and recognize that the weeks leading up to the Nativity of our Lord are *de facto* already the Christmas Season. Her proposal, as I remember it, was that we move Advent back to the beginning of November, retaining many of those end-time texts we hear anyway, and let that be our annual season of contemplating things eschatological with All Saints Day as its kick-off. There is something eminently reasonable about such a proposal, (especially for those of us, like myself, who used to be in campus ministry whose flocks had already dispersed by Christmas anyway!). But the bi-focal character of Advent—anticipating both the first coming of Jesus "at Christmastide in Bethlehem" and his second coming at the end of time—is a liturgical and pastoral challenge I'm not quite ready to give up. At least not yet.

Second Sunday in Advent

Psalm 85:1–2, 8–13
Isaiah 40:1–11
2 Peter 3:8–15a
Mark 1:1–8

Steadfast love and faithfulness will meet; righteousness
and peace will kiss one another.
Faithfulness will spring up from the ground, and
righteousness will look down from the sky.

—PSALM 85:10–11

Urgent Patience

Today's reading from 2 Peter is only one of two lections appointed in our *Revised Common Lectionary's* three-year cycle from this late, scarcely known part of the New Testament canon. It's become one of my favorite eschatological preaching texts as it combines allusions to several strains of end-time traditions. It begins with a musing reminiscent of the Hebrew wisdom tradition (cf. Psalm 90:4), *"Do not ignore this one fact, beloved, that with the Lord one day is like a thousand years, and a thousand years are like one day"* (v 8). The purpose for this philosophical observation, it soon becomes clear, is pastoral: *"The Lord is not slow concerning the promise, as some think of slowness, but is patient with you, not wanting any to perish but all to come to repentance"* (v 9). Evidently, as already in mid-century Thessalonica in Paul's day, so also in the community of saints to which 2 Peter was written, perhaps a half-century or more later, the seeming tardiness of God's promise-keeping was a matter that required pastoral care within the community of the faithful.

Following a reference common in eschatological literature, *"But the day of the Lord will come like a thief,"* come allusions to natural signs of the end, *"and then the heavens will pass away with a loud noise, and the elements will be dissolved with fire, and the earth and everything that is done on it will be disclosed"* (v 10). But it is in verse 11 that we encounter the question that lies simmering at the heart of all the language about watching and waiting and keeping awake and being prepared that we heard last week in our end-time texts: *"what sort of persons ought you to be in leading lives of holiness and godliness, waiting for and hastening the coming of the day of God"* (vv 11b–12a)? What sort of persons are we Advent people to be?

We are to be people of the promise is 2 Peter's answer, persons who trust and await the fulfillment of the promises of God: *"But in accordance with God's promise, we wait for new heavens and a new earth, where righteousness is at home"* (v 13). I love that phrase, *"where righteousness is at home"* (*"katoikei"* in Greek). This "homely" image of Jesus' coming at the end as a time, a place, a reality where God's righteousness will be *"at home,"* where God's justice is no longer alien but can kick off its shoes and put up its feet, helps give ethical content to our anticipation and waiting.

Our text concludes: *"Therefore, beloved, while you are waiting for these things strive to be found by God at peace, without spot or blemish; and regard the patience of our Lord as salvation"* (vv 14–15). What we Christians may be tempted to think of as God's slowness, the church's chronic and impatient lament at the so-called "delay of the *parousia*," is here transfigured into *"the patience* (literally, the "long-suffering") *of our Lord,"* which the church is urged to *"regard as salvation."* Hans Weder, in a seminal article entitled "Hope and Creation," has gone so far as to call for a far more "relaxed relation to the present"[3] including Christian ethical concerns on the basis of the genuine hope generated by God's end-time promises.

Many who hear today's first reading from Isaiah 40 can't help but do so to the strains of the opening tenor recitative, aria and chorus from Handel's *Messiah* sounding in their minds' ear.[4] But late Baroque is not Advent's only musical idiom. The fusion of text and melody, of music's ability to sing the gospel in the language of the heart, is particularly evident in the rich variety of Advent hymnody available to the church in our day. Many congregations, like the ones I served, annually host an Advent Service of Lessons and Carols that intersperses a number of Hebrew scripture and New Testament texts with Advent hymns and choral arrangements from a wide array of ethnic backgrounds and musical styles. None has been sung in recent years with greater vigor than Andraé Crouch's composed spiritual "Soon and Very Soon" (*ELW* #439). Both traditional Advent hymns, "On Jordan's Bank the Baptist's Cry," (*ELW* #249) and "Comfort, Comfort, Now My People" (*ELW* #256) provide good accompaniment to the Gospel reading for the day as well as containing echoes of Isaiah's paean of return that we hear read today, with its references to apocalyptic cataclysms of nature transfigured into a vision of the wilderness tamed, of valleys lifted up and mountains and hills made low, as a "highway for our God" is routed through the desert as Israel's way home.

Today's Gospel text from the very opening verses of Mark connects Isaiah's prophecy with *"the beginning of the good news of Jesus Christ, the Son of God"* (v 1) inaugurated with John the Baptizer's appearance in the wilderness, *"proclaiming a baptism of repentance for the forgiveness of sins"* (v 4). Yet John, whose exotic garb and diet easily identify him with the return of the prophet Elijah widely expected as a sign of the end time, is intent on underlining his own status as precursor rather than the main event: *"After me one who is more powerful than I is coming, the thong of*

---

3. In *The End of the World* ed. by Polkinghorne and Welker, 187–188. See also my essay, "The Wit to Relax", 115–121 which in an unedited version discusses Weder as well as the end-time texts the church hears on the ending and beginning Sundays of the church year.

4. See Bullard's *Messiah* as well as the excellent adult study resource by Reynolds, *Hallelujah: The Bible and Handel's Messiah.*

whose sandals I am not worthy to stoop down and untie. I have baptized you with water; but the one who is coming will baptize you with the Holy Spirit" (vv 7–8). Stay tuned, Mark's Gospel seems to be saying from the outset. You haven't seen anything yet!

Third Sunday of Advent

Psalm 126 or Luke 1:46b–55
Isaiah 61:1–4, 8–11
1 Thessalonians 5:16–24
John 1:6–8, 19–28

The Lord has done great things for us, and we rejoiced.

—Psalm 126:3

... the Mighty One has done great things for me, and holy is his name.

—Luke 1:49

Great Things

The prophet Isaiah's words, whose resonances are heard in Mary's song, begin with the text that is familiar from Jesus' reading of it during his visit to his hometown synagogue in Nazareth at the outset of his ministry as narrated in the fourth chapter of Luke's Gospel: "*The Spirit of the Lord God is upon me, because the Lord has appointed me . . . to bring good news . . . to bind up . . . to proclaim liberty . . . and release . . . to proclaim the year of the Lord's favor. . . to comfort all who mourn . . .* " (1–2). Here the prophet of Israel's return from exile sings a full-throated ode to joy that Jesus will adopt as the theme song for his ministry and agenda for his Spirit-fuelled mission: "*I will greatly rejoice in the Lord, my whole being shall exult in my God*" (v 10a). Apocalyptic gloom and doom and cataclysms of nature give way first to wedding imagery and then to a picture of Edenic life in a garden (remembering last week's reading from 2 Peter promising a time and place "*where righteousness is at home*"). "*For as the earth brings forth its shoots, and as a garden causes what is sown in it to spring up, so the Lord God will cause righteousness and praise to spring up before all the nations*" (v 11). The old and much-loved Swedish Advent hymn, "Rejoice, Rejoice, Believers" (*ELW* #244) weds text to music to create an unusually upbeat hymn of praise appropriate to today's texts.

"*Gaudete*," the Latin imperative for "rejoice," is the name by which this Third Sunday of Advent used to be known, supposedly because the Introit for the day began with a word of encouragement to joy, breaking into the theretofore penitential spirit for which Advent used to be known. Hence the lone pink candle that has hung on in some Advent wreaths. (I've always been suspicious that the change from penitential purple to hopeful blue and yet the retention of one pink candle had more to do with church publishing house marketing than liturgical scholarship, but who's to judge?) Anyway, both first and second readings do give strong encouragement to make this a day of rejoicing, and the readings generally represent a turn from the apocalyptic mood of the late November and early Advent readings to a more positive and confident attitude toward what Paul in 1 Thessalonians calls "*the coming of our Lord Jesus Christ*" (v 23b).[5] Use, if you're able, Paul's concluding words as your benediction for the day: "*May the God of peace himself sanctify you entirely; and may your spirit and soul and body be kept sound and blameless at the coming of our Lord Jesus Christ. The one who calls you is faithful, and he will do this*" (vv 23–24). Advent is a time to remember God's faithfulness which itself is the source of our faith-filled trust.

The Gospel reading begins with a snippet from the prologue to John's Gospel which refers to John the Baptizer as "*a man sent from God*" who came "*as a witness* ("martyr" in Greek) *to the light*" with the clear negation, also found in last week's Gospel reading from Mark 1, that "*he himself was not the light*" (vv 6–8). Then, jumping ten verses, we are given the Baptizer's own "*testimony*" that he is "*neither the Messiah, nor Elijah, nor the prophet*," but, invoking last week's text from Isaiah 40, "*I am the voice of one crying*

---

5. On joy as a Christian theme see two other essays in the book cited in the last postil, *The End of the World*, Miller's "Judgment and Joy," 155–170 and Wolf's "Enter into Joy!" 256–278.

out in the wilderness, 'Make straight the way of the Lord'" (v 23). This matter of what scholars call the "intertextuality of scripture," both the explicit citation and implicit resonances, echoes, and allusions of the older testament within the newer, and especially within Jesus' own teaching, is especially evident throughout our Advent texts and, as with the various Gospel passion accounts, is notably reliant on the Book of Isaiah.[6] "All Earth is Hopeful" (*ELW #266*) sings to a lively Hispanic tune of the joy that infuses this time of waiting as does the nearly contemporary hymn "There's a Voice in the Wilderness" (*ELW #255*).

Fourth Sunday of Advent

Luke 1:46b–55 or Psalm 89:1–4, 19–26
2 Samuel 7:1–11, 16
Romans 16:25–27
Luke 1:26–38

I will sing of your steadfast love, O Lord, forever;
with my mouth I will proclaim your faithfulness to all generations.

—PSALM 89:1

My soul magnifies the Lord, and my spirit rejoices in God my Savior . . .

—LUKE 1:47

Singing Mary's Song

Poised on the brink of Christmas, Advent finally relinquishes its bi-focal perspective on both the first and second comings of Christ and turns

---

6. Childs' *Isaiah* with its sensitivity to Isaiah's relationship to the whole canon of scripture, is here an excellent resource as a commentary.

full-face to consider the Davidic covenant's fulfillment in the angel's perplexing announcement to Mary. Her trusting response to the angel's annunciation became for Martin Luther the paradigmatic expression of faith: *"Here I am, the servant of the Lord; let it be with me according to your word"* (v 38). And Mary's song, *"Magnificat,"* sung in response to her visit to her relative Elizabeth (which is the alternative psalmody for today), becomes the archetypal psalm of faith. It echoes not only today's Psalm 89 but also Hannah's song (1 Samuel 2:1–10) and Miriam's/Moses' song (Exodus 15:1–20).

Luther's "Commentary on the *Magnificat*" written in 1521 during a time of one of the greatest outpourings of his most influential writings, merits a close reading.[7] Not only does it provide insight into Luther's exegetical acumen, but it affords homiletical and pastoral insights that are easily accessible to an adult study group. Here are a number of memorable nuggets: "this sacred hymn of the most blessed mother of God" (298); "God is the kind of Lord who does nothing but exalt those of low degree and put down the mighty from their thrones, in short, break what is whole and make whole what is broken" (299); "[Mary] sang it not for herself alone but for us all, to sing after her" (306); "being herself [Mary] no more than a cheerful guest chamber and willing hostess to so great a Guest" (308); "it is no less a miracle that she refrained from pride and arrogance . . . She finds herself the Mother of God, exalted above all mortals, and still remains so simple and so calm that she does not think of any poor serving maid as beneath her" (308).

And still more: "They delighted in their salvation much more than in their Savior, in the gift more than in the Giver, in the creature rather than the Creator" (309). "True humility . . . never knows that it is humble . . . for if it knew this, it would turn proud from contemplation of so fine a virtue" (315). ". . . there is today in the churches a great ringing of bells, blowing of trumpets, singing, shouting, and intoning, yet I fear precious little worship of God, who wants to be worshiped in spirit and truth, as he says in John 4:24" (325). "Mother of God. No one can say anything greater of her or to her, though he had as many tongues as there are leaves on the trees, or grass in the fields, or stars in the sky, or sand by the sea. It needs to be pondered in the heart what it means to be the Mother of God" (326). "We pray God to give us a right understanding of this *"Magnificat,"* an understanding that

---

7. *Luther's Works*, Vol. 21. The following quotations are each followed by its page reference.

consists not merely in brilliant words but in glowing life in body and soul. May Christ grant us this through the intercession and for the sake of His dear Mother Mary! Amen" (355).

Singing Mary's song after her is a good way of describing the church's everyday calling, but especially on this Sunday before Christmas. Numerous settings of "*Magnificat*" are available, of course, in the classical and contemporary repertoire, both solos and choral pieces, but the congregation should have an opportunity to join its collective voice in echoing Mary's words as well. Examples are *ELW* hymns #882, #573 and #251 as well as a paraphrase I'm partial to, "Canticle of the Turning" (*ELW* # 723), set to a lilting Irish melody. Others include chants #24 and #45 in Songs and Prayers from Taize and Marty Haugen's popular version from his *Holden Evening Prayer* which reminds us that "*Magnificat*" has for centuries served as the Gospel canticle for the church's vesper service and in monastic communities' services of evening prayer. But in addition, on this day when we hear of the annunciation to Mary, the lovely Basque carol, "The Angel Gabriel from Heaven Came" (*ELW* #265) must be sung as well as the lovely contemporary carol "Unexpected and Mysterious" (*ELW* #258) which in verse two sings, "In a momentary meeting of eternity and time,/Mary learned that she would carry both the mortal and divine,/Then she learned of God's compassion, of Elizabeth's great joy,/and she ran to greet the woman who would recognize her boy."

There is sufficient residual anti-Catholicism in many of us that attention to Mary's role in the incarnation can be thought reason for suspicion. As a young pastor, I remember being sternly advised by a retired clergyperson that the Advent meditation on Mary's "*Magnificat*" that I'd just presented to my fellow pastors was dangerously unevangelical, however much I quoted Luther on the matter. And indeed, some mariology can border on mariolatry.[8] Still, Mary as supreme exemplar of faith is a thoroughly evangelical idea, and as Luther himself said, "The Virgin birth is a mere trifle for God; that God should become man is a greater miracle; but most amazing of all is it that this maiden should credit the announcement that she, rather than some other virgin, had been chosen to be the mother of God."[9]

---

8. See publications of the US Lutheran–Roman Catholic Dialogue, *Mary in the New Testament* and *The One Mediator, the Saints and Mary* as well as Pelikan's, *Mary* to help discern the difference.

9. *Martin Luther Christmas Book*, ed. by Bainton 23.

Mary's trust in the angel's word was only possible by the gift of God's grace which enabled her to become "*theotokos*," "God-bearer," or "Mother of God," Luther's, along with the church fathers' (sic), favorite epithet for Mary. We could do worse than "ponder" this, as Luther said, and in our worship this day magnify our God who alone could accomplish such a miracle of faith.

SEASON OF CHRISTMAS

Nativity of Our Lord, Christmas Eve
(See Christmas Eve, Year A)

Nativity of Our Lord, Christmas Day
(See Christmas Day, Year A)

First Sunday of Christmas

Psalm 148
Isaiah 61:10—62:3
Galatians 4:4–7
Luke 2:22–40

Praise the Lord from the earth . . . fire and hail, snow and frost, stormy wind fulfilling his [God's] command!

—Psalm 148:7a, 8

A Tale of Two Crones

Sheer praise is the name of the game this Sunday so far as both our appointed psalmody and first reading from Third Isaiah are concerned. This is what I like to call "ecological doxology," nature's joining in God's praise as scripture often mentions and as legendary stories of Christmas like the "friendly beasts" who joined in adoration of the birth of the baby Jesus suggests, remnants of which remain in the old carol of the same name. For those living in northern climes it's reassuring to be reminded that hail, snow, frost, and stormy wind are not just grin'n' bear it realities of harsh winters. They can be imagined from the perspective of faith to be participants in creation's symphony of joy in praise of our Creator God. It's a stretch, but even the Catalonian carol, "Cold December Flies Away" (*ELW* #299)—how cold can it get in Catalonia, anyway?—encourages us to link today's warm basking in the afterglow of Christmas to the climatic and natural wonders of winter-time about us.

Isaiah's reference to Zion's vindication shining out "*like the dawn and its salvation like a burning torch*" (62:1b) entices us to expand our carol repertoire beyond our hymn books to include the likes of "Bring a Torch, Jeanette Isabella," a Provencal noel,[1] or the Galician carol, "Torches, Torches, Run With Torches."[2] If we're fastidious about delaying the singing of Christmas carols until Christmas has arrived, now is the time to bring them all out in this all-too-brief season of rejoicing.

Luke 2 points the way for our delight in Jesus' birth by preserving for the church both the poignant story and precious song contained in these few verses that flesh out what Paul in our second reading refers to in the closest thing to a Christmas narrative he ever wrote: "*When the fullness of time had come, God sent the Son, born of a woman, born under the law, in order to redeem those who were under the law, so that we might receive adoption as children*" (Gal 4:4–5). Fidelity to what it meant to be "*born under the law*" is what led Mary and Joseph to bring their infant son to the temple in Jerusalem "*to present him to the Lord*" according to the "*law*," a word Luke considers sufficiently important to mention five times.

Awaiting them in the temple were two "old crones," as we might call them. The first, Simeon, was a man "*righteous and devout, looking forward to the consolation of Israel*," but Luke adds portentously, "*and the Holy Spirit rested on him*." Not only that, but the Spirit had revealed to him "*that he would not see death before he had seen the Lord's Messiah*." Guided by this same Spirit, Simeon, in a moment of divine coincidence, came into the temple as his "*parents*" presented Jesus "*to do for him what was customary under the law*," peremptorily took the child in his arms (vv 25–28) and burst into the lyrical words of "*Nunc Dimittis*" (described further below). And then, in an effort at equal opportunity, following Simeon's poignant blessing, the other "crone" appears, "*a prophet Anna*" who Luke bothers to tell

---

1. *Noels*, 136.
2. *Oxford Book of Carols*, 176.

us *"never left the temple but worshipped there with fasting and prayer night and day."* She too *"began to praise God and to speak about the child to all who were looking for the redemption of Jerusalem"* (vv 36–38).[3]

The "Song of Simeon," called *"Nunc Dimittis"* from its first two words in Latin, is the third of the poetic songs or canticles that Luke has included in the first two chapters of his Gospel (or fourth if the angel's song to the shepherds, *"Gloria in Excelsis"* [Luke 2:14] is counted, as I think it should be!). Each has found a home in the various liturgies of the church. *"Nunc Dimittis"* is sung at Compline (Prayer at the Close of the Day) and in the order for the Burial of the Dead. It is also given as an optional post-communion canticle in the order for Holy Communion and is especially fitting to be sung on these Sundays after Christmas. Tillis Butler's and James Harris's "Now, Lord, You Let Your Servant Go in Peace" originally found in the "Detroit Folk Mass," is a wonderfully bluesy setting now reprinted in *ELW* as #200.

I remember years ago a friend receiving a Christmas card from the noted church historian and biographer of Luther, Roland Bainton, who was known as an inveterate caricaturist (I have a couple cartoons he once did of me that are far from flattering!). Bainton had sketched a drawing of Simeon holding the baby Jesus in his arms, and then had written: "Simeon, the aged, held the baby Jesus, one would assume, for less than a quarter of an hour. Yet he could say that he had seen a light for revelation." Bainton, himself in his eighties at the time, went on poignantly: "Life is so full of brief encounters. Some of you, my friends, once close, I have not seen for all of sixty years. But the impact is not to be measured in length of days. Cherished memories and annual greetings are an inalienable blessing."

How much poorer the church would be if Luke had not included this little, lyrically recounted tale of Joseph's and Mary's intentions to do *"everything required by the law of the Lord"* (v 39a) and of the role of the faithful attendance on their actions by two ancient yet contemporary prophets of their faith, Simeon and Anna. (This is also the Gospel text assigned for "The Presentation of our Lord" which falls on February 2—Ground Hog's Day, in secular parlance.)

Should "Holy Innocents, Martyrs," which falls on December 28 be observed, special note should be taken of Simeon's admonitory warning to Mary about Jesus' destiny and his puzzling but ominous words that *"a sword will pierce your own soul too"* (vv 34–35). Here the shadow of the

---

3. For more on widows and Anna's larger significance see Thurston's *Widows*, 22–35.

cross is cast backward upon the beginning of Jesus' story in the horrible tale of the mass murder of the Bethlehem babies, a true "menacing of Christmas," as I've already observed (see First Sunday after Christmas, Year A). "Oh, Sleep Now, Holy Baby" (*With One Voice*, #639) is a lovely Hispanic folk song that sings the reassurance "You need not fear King Herod, he will bring no harm to you."

Second Sunday of Christmas
(See Second Sunday of Christmas, Year A)

Epiphany of Our Lord
(See Epiphany of Our Lord, Year A)

TIME AFTER EPIPHANY

Baptism of Our Lord, First Sunday after Epiphany, Lectionary 1

Psalm 29
Genesis 1:1–5
Acts 19:1–7
Mark 1:4–11

The voice of the Lord is over the waters ; the God of glory thunders . . . over mighty waters. The voice of the Lord is powerful; the voice of the Lord is full of majesty.

—Psalm 29:3–4

Torn Curtain

Mark's Gospel has no proper Christmas story—no Bethlehem manger, no angel chorus, no magi from the East. Instead Mark begins his Gospel with John's appearance in the wilderness culminating in Jesus' baptism by John. This suggests that if we had only Mark's Gospel we might assume that Jesus became the Son of God at his baptism as he saw the heavens ripped apart and the Spirit descending upon him like a dove while hearing the words: "*You are my Son, the beloved; with you I am well pleased*" (v 11). I always think what a gift it is to the church how each of the four Gospels tells the good news of Jesus from quite different, and yet, I'd argue, complementary perspectives underlining the theme of diversity with which the church finds it so hard to live.[1] And even more amazing, perhaps, is the fact that the church found a way to allow this diversity to be canonized, even while excluding certain other ancient writings that may have been candidates for inclusion. While all four Gospels judge the story of Jesus' baptism as important to the overall gospel narrative, Mark's placing it front and center helps us to see how absolutely crucial Jesus' baptism was—and by implication, ours as well—to the story of salvation.

Without subscribing to the ancient heresy of "adoptionism," that is, Jesus becoming the Son of God at his baptism, I think it is helpful to pay close attention to Mark's account and how it, in a sense, renders its own take on the implications of Jesus as God's foray into the mysteries of incarnation—of what it means for God to have become fully human in the person of Jesus without resort to genealogies, annunciations, and birth stories.

We can begin by giving credit to the authors of the lectionary in putting before us today as our first reading the first five verses of the Bible, from Genesis, the book of beginnings. Here we encounter the primitive story of the *"ruah"* of God (wind, breath, spirit) sweeping over the face of the formless watery chaos and speaking light into being. *"Let there be light"* and there was light, by God's very speaking of the creative Word. What's more, Genesis says, *"God saw that the light was good,"* a judgment, we know from the rest of the story, that God will repeat several times until at the ultimate creation of humankind in God's own image, the Creator will look out over all creation judging it to be *"very good"* (vv 3–4, 31). Here at the near outset of Mark's Gospel we are encountered by this same hovering Spirit as a voice from above articulates its pleasure over what is occurring, as Jesus emerges spluttering from the waters of the Jordan in which John had dunked him. And so, Mark's "Christmas story," if you want to call it that, is not about the birth of the baby Jesus at all. Rather, it is the story of Jesus being "born anew" via the watery womb of baptism emerging into the affirmation of God's voice and the Spirit's warm embrace.

But for Mark—the tersest of the Gospels—there's a crucial detail in his telling of the story to which we need to pay attention, a detail easily concealed in these seemingly innocuous words: *"and as Jesus was coming up out of the water, he saw the heavens torn apart and the Spirit descending upon him like a dove"* (v 10). It's the biblical scholar Donald Juel who, to my mind, best plumbs the depths of this matter in his work on Mark including

---

1. See here Rhoads, *Challenge of Diversity,* 60–78.

his *Master of Surprise: Mark Interpreted* and in his commentary entitled *Mark*. Most of what follows derives from Juel's work beginning with his exegetical observations regarding the verb in the passage just cited translated in the *NRSV* as "*torn apart.*" The older *RSV* had under-translated the Greek word "*schizomenous*" with the bland "*the heavens were opened,*" a word that has a much sharper edge that connotes a "violent division" or a "cutting apart," a "splitting" or even "ripping open," as is suggested by its English derivatives including words like "schism" or "schizophrenia" or even, simply, "scissors."[2]

Juel points out that a form of this rather violent Greek word occurs once again near the very end of Mark's Gospel, the two serving symbolically as a sort of "bookends" to Mark's telling of the Jesus' story. This second occurrence is among the words we'll read together in Mark's passion story at the beginning of this coming Holy Week, when at its very climax we will hear Jesus utter those most heart-rending and soul-chilling words from the cross, Jesus' only words from the cross in Mark's telling of the tale, "*My God, my God, why have you forsaken me?*" Then, Mark says, "*Jesus gave a loud cry and breathed his last.*" It's then that we hear what we can be forgiven for thinking as these puzzling, almost anti-climactic words, "*And the curtain of the temple was torn in two from top to bottom*" (15:34, 37–38).[3]

So what, you ask? Well, here's what, according to Donald Juel. The curtain of the temple, he explains, referred most likely to the drapery which separated the Holy of Holies, the place where God was symbolically present, from the rest of the temple sanctuary. This was the sacred precinct where the ark of the covenant was kept out of bounds from all mortals except the high priest, who was allowed to enter it only once a year on the Day of Atonement, what Jews today call "Yom Kippur." The curtain, it was thought, provided protection from God's holy presence, for that presence could mean death for any who encountered it directly.[4]

But in addition, Juel explains, the temple was fitted with another veil, a larger piece of cloth that served as a kind of door in the summer when the massive gates were left open. This veil was embroidered with cosmic imagery, symbolizing an association with the heavens as themselves a kind of cosmic scrim. The Jewish historian Josephus, a contemporary of the

---

2. Juel, *Master of Surprise*, 34.
3. Ibid., 34–35.
4. Ibid., 35.

first generation of Christians, describes this curtain at the entrance to the temple as follows (which is worth quoting at length):

> Before these hung a veil of equal length, of Babylonian tapestry, with embroidery of blue and fine linen, of scarlet also and purple wrought with marvelous skill. Nor was this mixture of materials without its mystic meaning: it typified the universe. For the scarlet seemed emblematic of fire, the fine linen of the earth, the blue of the air, and the purple of the sea... On this tapestry was portrayed a panorama of the heavens...[5]

So, Juel surmises, the image of a curtain or veil suggests that "the ripping of the temple veil" might be meant by Mark to be interpreted as symbolizing that something is finished with Jesus' last breath that was begun with Jesus' first gasp for air as he came up out of the Jordan when the heavens themselves are described as having been "ripped open," "torn apart," when the Spirit descended like a dove even as the voice from the newly rent heavens declared its delight in Jesus. It may mean, Juel suggests further, as the Letter to the Hebrews puts it in quasi-cultic language, that we now have access to God in a new way as we can now "*have confidence to enter the sanctuary by the blood of Jesus*" (10:19). A pattern that began with Jesus' baptism now ends with his death. If the heavens are merely "opened" as in Matthew's and Luke's Gospels and in earlier translations of Mark, then they may well close again. But if they are "torn apart" or "ripped open" then we may think of some permanent damage or rupture that cannot be repaired.[6]

This is why, at Juel's instigation, I've come to think that the baptism of Jesus is really Mark's re-imagined version of the Christmas story, as God "tears open" the vault of the sky which was traditionally thought to separate heaven and earth in the ancient world's "three-story universe," in which God's dwelling place in heaven was separated from the created order where humanity dwelt. To put it another way, this suggests that in Jesus, humanity's domain of the created order was invaded by God, as the voice was heard and the Spirit descended upon Jesus at his baptism through the "ripped open" heavens, a ripping open that was repeated and made permanent in Jesus' death on the cross when God in Christ signaled full solidarity with us human ones even in our death. The torn curtain of the temple, as the ripping apart of the heavens, symbolizes that God is unwilling to be confined to "sacred spaces" but is rather "on the loose" in our earthly realm,

5. Josephus, *Jewish Wars* cited in Juel, *Master of Surprise*, 35.
6. Ibid., 34–36

on the loose in the form of the Spirit present at creation now descended "into"—not just "upon"—Jesus, as Juel insists. Jesus, we're to understand, is a man "possessed" as his opponents kept accusing him of being, but he is one possessed by God's Spirit.[7] The contemporary hymn, "Crashing Waters at Creation" (*ELW* #455) nicely combines references to the Spirit's presence at creation as at Jesus' baptism—and ours.

Second Sunday after Epiphany, Lectionary 2

(Martin Luther King, Jr. Commemoration)
Psalm 139:1–6, 13–18
1 Samuel 3:1–10 [11–20]
1 Corinthians 6:12–20
John 1:43–51

I praise you for I am fearfully and wonderfully made.
Wonderful are your works; that I know very well.

—Psalm 139:14

Come and See

Isn't it remarkable that on this day on which the church commemorates the life, witness and vision of Dr. Martin Luther King Jr., that almost the first words we hear from our appointed Hebrew scripture reading from the First Book of Samuel are: "*In those days, the Word of God was rare and visions were not widespread*" (v 1b)? In "those days," huh? Have things really changed that much in the three millennia since Samuel's day? Or in the nearly fifty years since brother Martin's martyrdom, just weeks before my graduation from college in the spring of 1968? We remember, with nostalgia, Martin's words delivered in front of the Lincoln Memorial, five years before his assassination, about his having a dream. As he so memorably

---

7. Ibid., 36.

put it, "in spite of the difficulties and frustrations of the moment I still have a dream . . . a dream," he claimed, that is "deeply rooted in the American dream . . . a dream that my four little children will one day live in a nation where they will not be judged by the color of their skin but by the content of their character." (See my postil for Year A, Epiphany 2, for more on M. L. King, Jr., including a story of his own "call.") Well, dream on, Martin, we sigh, as racism continues to raise its ugly head, what's been called "America's original sin." But we dream too, don't we? For we know that Martin's dream wasn't just a private vision, nor even one rooted only in the American dream, even in that vision set to paper in the US Constitution and its Bill of Rights.

But brother Martin's dream was one that he also claimed, of course, was one inspired by God's Word and rooted in the scriptures. Visions, you see, authentic God-given visions, are a double-edged gift from God. Because seeing things as they really are meant to be—and will be, by God's promise—casts a whole new light on things as we now experience them and are used to seeing them. For some of us, like Nathaniel of our Gospel reading, it may be difficult to set aside our world-weary cynicism which we like to call "being realistic." *Can anything good come out of Nazareth?"* Nathaniel sneers in response to his excitable friend Philip's news, bubbling over with enthusiasm: *"We've found him about whom Moses in the law and also the prophets wrote, Jesus son of Joseph from Nazareth."* Nathaniel's snide response is perhaps the most cutting put-down in all of scripture, and so bears repeating in its utter world-weariness, *"Can anything good come out of Nazareth?"* (vv 45–46a).

Sometimes I—and I bet, you too—find myself behaving like Nathaniel, as a new idea or a fresh insight is shared with me. Oh, I'm rarely as blunt as Nathaniel in throwing cold water on another's enthusiasm or in making fun of someone's excitement about a new idea. But I'm afraid that too often, I'm just as dismissive and skeptical in my own (pastorally sensitive) way. The older I get, I fear, the more easily I assume that I've seen it all before, we've tried that before, so what's the use? I find myself as enslaved as anyone to those famous "seven last words" of the church: "We've never done it that way before!" or even worse, "Oh, we already tried that once before."

But our Gospel text doesn't end, I hope you noticed, with Nathaniel's curt dismissal. I think Philip's reply is instructive and illuminating for us—even a kind of epiphany or vision in itself—as to how we might respond to those who pour cold water on others' visions and ideas. What is Philip's response? He simply tells his sarcastic buddy, *"Come and see!"* No evidence that he's taken offense at Nathaniel's slur personally. He doesn't feel the need to get mad or get even or start an argument. The casualness of his response I find astounding. Philip simply says, *"Come and see!"*

I've come to see (been given the vision?) that this, in essence, is what true evangelism is all about (as we'll hear more of in next week's story from Mark's Gospel of Jesus' calling of the disciples away from their fishnets to come and follow him). Proclaiming the good news of Jesus is really just a matter of a word-of-mouth invitation to another person—especially a person you care about—to *"come and see."* Come and see for yourself who this Jesus is and what he's all about. We, the church, aren't saying "come and see us"—what a lively, intelligent, politically correct, non-racist and generally interesting group of people we are—a religious club that any right-minded person would be proud to belong to (see Paul in 1 Corinthians 1:26–31 e.g.). What we're saying is *"come and see"* not us but the one in whose name we gather, at whose font we wash, at whose table we eat, and in whose name we scatter to live out our daily lives in service to the world—like Dr. Martin Luther King Jr. and other Christians, known and unknown, through the ages who understand their calling, their vision, to be transparent to Jesus, to be those earthen vessels God is molding, cracked though we be, through whom the light of Christ becomes visible. Or to use Paul's terms in today's second reading, we are those called by God to consider our own bodies—flesh and blood, warts and all—as temples of the Holy Spirit which, Paul insists, *"you have from God"* with the clear implication that *"you are not your own"* for *"you were bought with a price"* (vv 19–20). Now that's a rare vision with which even the Psalmist of old concurs!

The Tanzanian hymn "Listen, God is Calling" (*ELW* #513) offers a fitting introduction to the story of the boy Samuel's calling by God with a nice call and response dialogue between leader and people. "Here I Am, Lord" (*ELW* #574) makes the boy Samuel's reply our refrain. For any M.L. King, Jr. commemoration James Weldon Johnson's "Lift Every Voice and Sing" (*ELW* #841) needs to be sung but consider also the ancient Celtic hymn, "Be Thou My Vision," (*ELW* #793).

Year B

Third Sunday after Epiphany, Lectionary 3

Psalm 62:5–12
Jonah 3:1–5, 10
1 Corinthians 7:29–31
Mark 1:14–20

*Once God has spoken, twice have I heard this:
that power belongs to God, and steadfast love belongs to you, O Lord.*

—Psalm 62:11–12a

Life Change

Today's readings from scripture point to the change of heart and mind that is crucial to being a Christian and being church together. It's that "repentance" which Jonah was called by God to provoke in the Ninevites which led to Jonah's own eventual repentance, his coming around to accepting the fact that indeed God was a God of mercy as well as justice, "*a gracious God and merciful, slow to anger, and abounding in steadfast love, and ready to relent from punishing*" (Jonah 4:2, see the postil for Year A, Lectionary 25 for more on Jonah). Jonah, you see, had to repent of his own resentment over God's willingness to forgive which led him to flee from God's call in the first place, fearing that God would lead the Ninevites to repent—which they did!

It's also "repentance" which our Gospel text for today tells us was Jesus' essential message at the outset of his ministry, as it had been John the Baptizer's before him (who had now been arrested, our text tells us). "*Jesus came to Galilee, proclaiming the good news of God,*" Mark informs us, "*and saying, 'The time is fulfilled, and the kingdom of God has come near; repent, and believe in the good news.'*" The Greek word for "repentance," "*metanoia*," my lexicon tells me, means a "change of heart," a "turning from one's sins," a "change of way" all of which I think are well comprehended in Eugene Peterson's choice of "life change" as his favored translation in his contemporary paraphrase of the Bible called *The Message*. "*Repent, and believe in the good news*" is Jesus' message followed by his simple command to Simon and Andrew whom he found casting a net into the sea: "*Follow me and I will make you fish for people*"—or "*fishers of men*" as the RSV used to translate more felicitously, if less inclusively.

Here I've decided to depart from the usual generality of my interpretation of the text for the purpose of preaching to suggest a very particular example from my own pastoral ministry that I've used to demonstrate both God's gift of repentance as "life change" as well as our—and especially the church's—dire need for repentance over the church's teaching and rule-making regarding the issue of homosexuality. It's a real-life story that I hope you'll find compelling and revelatory of the implications of today's texts regarding "repentance" as "life change." I've altered names and places to protect the confidentiality of those involved.

Not long before leaving the parish I had served for several years for a new call in a new state I received a phone call from a retired bishop with whom I was slightly acquainted. He knew of my involvement with glbt issues within the church and was calling me as a potential resource for a relative of his who lived in my area who had a sixteen year old son who, he said, was gay and suffering from depression. He said a bit more about the situation that I needn't detail here, wondering if I'd be willing to serve as a pastoral resource and counsel and possible referral for the boy and his mother. I said I'd be glad to try, and we left it that he would have them get in touch with me directly.

The next day the boy's mother called (let's call her Angie), and thanked me for my willingness to help. She immediately poured out to me her son's story, which, I was glad to hear, included her own strong affirmation and acceptance of his gay self-identity which, she said, he'd come to as long before as age twelve. Since that time he'd disclosed his sexual orientation to only a handful of those closest to him as well as the therapist who was working with him. But for some time her son ("Bob" let's call him) had been suffering from depression including thoughts of suicide, as he had been continuing to keep his secret from kids at school and the youth group at his church where he and his mother were very active. Bob, she went on, had recently gotten up the courage to talk with his own pastor who had patiently listened to Bob's self-disclosure but was utterly unable to offer Bob any assurance of God's acceptance of his being gay. Bob needed such assurance, Angie told me, but his pastor had been unwilling, or perhaps theologically unable, to offer Bob such affirmation. "Can you Pastor?" she pleaded with me. "I certainly can,"

I responded but, of course, couldn't help wondering whether her son could take my word for it as someone he had never met. We left it that she would check out Bob's willingness to meet with me, and a few days later the three of us found ourselves sitting around a table in a diner near their hometown.

Bob was indeed a great kid and I could tell right away that Angie was just the kind of mom a kid would need to get through this (Angie's a single mother). After getting acquainted, Angie left so we could talk privately. Bob shared his story with me after which I let him know a bit about myself and what I thought the Bible has to say on the matter of homosexuality and how, in my opinion, the church is all too slowly learning to change its mind on these issues. He told me how tough it's been for him at school and church and how he's haunted not so much by suicidal thoughts—he loves his mother so deeply, he said, that he'd promised her he'd never do anything to himself—and yet he confessed that sometimes the thought of death was very consoling to him because of all the trouble he feels he's causing others. I dropped him off at his home, leaving a few written resources I'd brought along and urged him to keep in touch. An idea I left with him was that it might be good for him to meet some gay and lesbian folks further along the road of life who'd been through what he was experiencing. I offered to put him in touch with members of my own congregation, people of faith who'd be willing to share their stories.

To make a long story shorter, a couple of days later I received an email from Angie who thanked me very much for my visit and asked me to keep Bob in my prayers. She confessed: "I'm very sad today" as she went on to say how Bob had "flat-lined" and how his depression had become "deeper and more all-pervasive than I have ever seen." So now too I was depressed. A lot of help I'd been! A few days later I received another email from Angie telling me how folks at Bob's school had become alarmed at his slide into depression and how after a meeting with Bob's therapist they'd acted immediately to get him into an adolescent treatment facility in a nearby city.

The next email a couple of days later told an amazing story—as amazing as the astonishing repentance of the Ninevites in response to Jonah's preaching or the fishermen's willingness to leave their nets to follow Jesus. Bob, Angie reported, while still at the treatment facility had gone to lie down on his bed for a few minutes to listen to a favorite Christian music cd she'd just dropped off for him. He reported how he was pretty sure he'd fallen asleep but only twenty seconds had passed on his boom box during which, he testified, "God came to me. He really came to me." Bob didn't remember the specific words he heard but, he said, "He confirmed everything that I've been doubting about myself for the past several years. It's not a sin that I'm gay. He didn't make any mistake when he made me. I feel really good." And so, of course, did I! At Angie's urging I phoned Bob to share with him my delight in the Word of affirmation he felt he'd received from God.

Several days passed until I received what turned out to be my penultimate email from Angie (since I was in the throes of leaving for a new call) in which she recounted a meeting between Bob and his teachers and principal at school which she'd also attended. The principal had started by telling Bob how important he was to all those in the room and Bob in turn shared with the whole room the story of what had been depressing him for the past several years and how difficult it was to be a closeted gay teenager in high school. "I just about gave him a standing ovation," his mother wrote. Two teachers came up and gave him hugs and others kept him after class to tell him how proud they were of him. "So, all in all, the day really couldn't have gone any better . . . " she concluded.

I don't know the rest of Bob's story, these many years later. My last email from Angie was simply a thank you and farewell for my having been "a real blessing in our lives." Little as I knew I'd done, and unfinished as Bob's story was, I was grateful to be thanked. But for me Bob's story, as far as I knew it, was the real gift to me. If Bob's got a long way to go, it's not nearly so far as the church has to go in its need for repentance, for true life change. I can't help but think of Bob's pastor whom I don't know and can't pretend to be in any position to judge. But I can't help but wonder if both the church (and its bishops) and the pastor might be guilty of pastoral malpractice in a matter with such life and death consequences.

I know that this story about repentance and true life change may not be compelling to all who will read it. But I think today's texts including Jesus' call to repentance and to follow him in becoming "fishers of people" all constitute together the good news Jesus came to embody and proclaim, good news that leads to genuine "life change," change of minds and hearts.

John Bell's "The Summons" also known by its first line as "Will You Come and Follow Me?" fits perfectly today's texts, especially in verse 4 where it asks, "Will you love the you you hide if I but call your name?/ Will you quell the fear inside and never be the same?" (*ELW* #798). "You Have Come Down to the Lakeshore" (*ELW* #817) is a lovely Hispanic hymn translated liltingly by a good friend, Madeline Forell Marshall. Sing a verse or two in Spanish as well.

Year B

Fourth Sunday after Epiphany, Lectionary 4

Psalm 111
Deuteronomy 18:15–20
1 Corinthians 8:1–13
Mark 1:21–28

*Great are the works of the Lord, studied by all who delight in them . . .
The fear of the Lord is the beginning of wisdom . . .*

—PSALM 111:2, 10A

Author-ity

Mark, if nothing else, is an unusually economic and even terse story teller. And so immediately following upon Jesus' call to the Galilean fisher folk to leave their nets and *"follow me"* which we heard last week, Jesus and his disciples find themselves, in the very next verse, in Capernaum, a city on the Sea of Galilee which in Mark's Gospel seems to be the headquarters of Jesus and his rag-tag following. It's the sabbath, Mark tells us, and with no whys or wherefores simply informs us that *"he entered the synagogue and taught,"* immediately following which, he adds, *"They were astounded at his teaching."* Mark, of course, has told us nothing of Jesus' preparation to be a teacher, save the story of his baptism when he was suddenly "possessed" by God's Holy Spirit while hearing the affirming voice of God from on high. And, oh yes, there was that forty day temptation in the wilderness that immediately followed (which we'll hear about on Lent 1) that certainly was a preparation of sorts! But while piquing our curiosity about what might have prepared Jesus to be such an astonishing teacher, Mark doesn't leave us clueless as to why his teaching was perceived to be so astonishing, *"For he taught them as one having authority, and not as the scribes"* (v 21–22), Mark thinks it important to tell us.

Beginning, for once, with the English word "authority," I like to parse the word to its origin in the word "author," which my dictionary defines as "a person who makes or originates something; creator; instigator." "Authority," then, is the power or aura that flows from an author, as "creativity" from a "creator." (True confession: I've used this text to celebrate "authors" and their peculiar gift to the church and the world, once making mention of a particularly gifted playwright who was a member of one of the congregations I served, as well as celebrating the work of the well known author and onetime Lutheran, John Updike, who had recently died.) The Greek word "*exousia,*" which is translated as "authority," is a word widely used in the synoptics in connection with Jesus where, while "authority" is its favored connotation, it can also mean "right," "liberty," "ability," "capability" and "supernatural or ruling power." I stress the apt implications in English of "authority" deriving from "author" because I think it nicely carries the sense that there is a certain creative charisma deriving from the person of Jesus the teacher who is authentically the "originator" of what he is saying in a way that differed from "the scribes" whose authority had to do with the written word or scripture. Here, I think we see from the outset of Jesus' ministry that there is something different about Jesus' teaching, which we'll see certainly takes scripture into account but often moves beyond the letter to the spirit of the law, reinterpreting it in light of what Jesus will call "the kingdom of God."

But what makes this first encounter with the authority of Jesus' teaching particularly significant is what follows. For there happened to be in the synagogue that day, Mark tells us, *"a man with an unclean spirit"* who immediately confronts Jesus and his authority crying, *"What have you to do with us, Jesus of Nazareth?"* (Here I've sometimes told the story from my child-hood of how the little village church in which I was raised had a "mad man" named Arnie who lived next door above the general store where he tended the goat herd in the barn behind the store. Arnie wasn't a regular at worship but would occasionally appear in his dirty and smelly clothes, reeking of alcohol which was probably his way of medicating his mental illness, whatever that may have been. For us kids he was both a scary character and a relief from our regular church routine. He absolutely terrified our young pastor's wife who lived in the parsonage across the street. We've all had some experience of people "acting out" in church or of being visited by folks of unstable mental condition, known or unknown, and are familiar with the dis-ease such folks' presence immediately creates within the congregation, not to say ushers and clergy!) But this *"man with the unclean"* spirit wasn't content to merely confront

Jesus' authority. "*Have you come to destroy us?*" he asks, the plural pronoun perhaps mystifying us and the original crowd of synagogue-goers. But he continues even more inexplicably , "*I know who you are, the Holy One of God,*"(vv 23–24), the first acknowledgement in Mark's Gospel by someone of who Jesus "authoritatively" is, although textual sleuths will have noticed that the man somehow knew Jesus' name and place of origin already at his initial outburst.

"*But Jesus rebuked him,*" Mark tell us, a strong word in Greek that can simply mean "commanded" or "scolded." Jesus is clearly taking charge as he commands (with authority) "*Be silent, and come out of him*" (v 25). Some suggest this could be translated more rudely, "Shut up and get outta' here," except the pronoun clearly means "get outta' *him*." And, Mark reports, "*the unclean spirit* (note singular), *convulsing him and crying with a loud voice, came out of him.*" Whether this suggests the diagnosis that the "unclean man" was an epileptic, a broad diagnosis still today, we don't know, but it's significant that in the course of the story the "unclean man" had become an "unclean spirit." The clear implication is that the man had been "inhabited" or, as we earlier said of Jesus and the Spirit, "possessed" by an "unclean spirit," and was not culpable for his earlier behaviors. No more is heard of him.

Only the response of the synagogue-goers is reported. "*They were all amazed, and* (with a nice feel for dramaturgy, Mark informs us) *they kept on asking one another, 'What is this? A new teaching—with authority! He commands even the unclean spirits, and they obey him'*" (vv 25–27). And so we return to Jesus' authority, here expanded to include the connotation of "power," the potency to produce action as well as wield authority. It is not unconnected to Jesus' authoritative teaching now given the label of "a new teaching," novelty certainly being something to which no one would have accused the scribes of aspiring! And Mark appends this afterword regarding Jesus' first ministry foray: "*At once his fame began to spread throughout the surrounding region of Galilee*" (v 28). Yep, I bet it did, a matter Jesus will soon need to combat in his insistence on keeping the "messianic secret" so dear to Mark. "When Pain of the World Surrounds Us" (*ELW* #704) sings of our need to let God's "healing" and "changes" flow through us.

Fifth Sunday after Epiphany, Lectionary 5

Psalm 147:1–11, 20c
Isaiah 40:21–31
1 Corinthians 9:16–23
Mark 1:29–39

Great is our Lord, and abundant in power;
his understanding is beyond measure.

—Psalm 147:5

Grasshoppers?

All of our texts for today, despite their considerable dissimilarities, have this in common: they presume that faith has a *"message"* to *"proclaim,"* as Mark says of Jesus; that Paul has a *"gospel to proclaim"* as he writes the church at Corinth; or as our psalm puts it, we have *"thanksgiving and praise to sing"* in response to the Creator God *"who sends out his word; who makes the wind to blow and the waters to flow."* There is a message, a proclamation, a gospel, a word that draws us together and sends us out as church.

But today let our Hebrew scripture reading from Isaiah 40 take the lead, that same chapter from which we heard the beautiful if familiar words back in Advent, *"Comfort, o, comfort my people, says your God. Speak tenderly to Jerusalem and cry to her . . . "* (40:1–2a) as well as those words that John the Baptizer would cite which he saw in reference to his own ministry in the wilderness: *"the voice of one crying out in the wilderness: 'Prepare the way of the Lord, make his paths straight'"* (Mark 1:2 quoting Isaiah 40:6).

It's just a bit further on in this much-loved fortieth chapter of Isaiah that the words of today's text are found, words perhaps not quite as familiar to most of us. But they're words at whose literary/oratorical impact I marvel as the passage begins with a series of seemingly relentless rhetorical questions that drive us, the hearers, to the point of awed silence: *"Have you not seen? Have you not known? Has it not been told you from the beginning? Have you not understood from the foundations of the earth?" (v 21).*

It hushes us up, doesn't it? And maybe puts us a bit on the defensive? What is it we're supposed to have known, heard, been told? What is it we're to have understood from the *"foundations of the earth,"* that was told us *"from the beginning?"* Get ready now! *"It is God who sits above the circle of the earth and its inhabitants* (that includes you and me, so listen carefully now): *"its inhabitants are like grasshoppers."* That's it? That's the message, the Word, the good news, that God has for us—that we're *"like grasshoppers?!"* Well, how does that make you feel? Why, I thought we were created in God's image. I thought we humans were inspired by the very breath of God breathed into us at creation. I thought, as the psalmist put it, that we're made just a *"little lower than the angels,"* and, what's more, that God has given us *"dominion"* over all things. So how is it we're grasshoppers?

But the message, the Word, the good news isn't, in fact, so much about us, in the first place, as it is about God. But mention us, us human grasshoppers, and that's all we hear with our anthropocentric way of hearing and seeing and understanding. So let's back up a minute and hear it all again as a good word about God: *"Have you not known? Have you not heard? Has it not been told you from the beginning? Have you not understood from the foundations of the earth? It is God who sits above the circle of the earth, and its inhabitants are like grasshoppers, who* (that is "God") *stretches out the heavens like a curtain, and spreads them like a tent to live in; who brings the great to naught and makes the rulers of the earth as nothing"* (vv 21–22). Take that, "masters of the universe," whether in Washington or Moscow, Tel Aviv or Teheran, Bejing or Silicon Valley! And the prophet concludes, altering the image: *"Scarcely are they planted, scarcely sown, scarcely has their stem taken root in the earth, when God blows upon them and they wither, and the tempest carries them off like stubble"* (v 2).

The English Catholic writer of the early twentieth century, G.K. Chesterton, author of the Father Brown mysteries and caustic Christian apologist, once observed that there are essentially two kinds of people in the world: when trees are waving wildly in the wind, one group thinks that it is the wind that moves the trees while the other group thinks that the motion of the trees creates the wind. Most of humankind, Chesterton goes on, through most of the centuries of human history has believed that the wind moves the trees. But in recent, more modern times, a new breed of people has emerged who hold that it is the movement of the trees that creates the wind.

Now what Chesterton is getting at is that the older consensus always held that the *invisible* is behind and gives energy to the *visible*. But in our modern, "secular" world this former broad consensus has fallen apart in a world dominated by what we like to think of as the enlightened scientific world view, so that today what most people naively assume they see and hear and touch—what is measurable and quantifiable—is the "really real— and it is this so-called "empirical" reality which generates whatever people come up with that cannot be verified with the senses. But as Paul wrote the Romans, "*For in hope we were saved. Now hope that is seen is not hope. For who hopes for what is seen?*" Or as he wrote the Corinthians, "*we walk by faith, not by sight*" (Rom 8:24 and 2 Cor 5:7). Like the wind, whose effects we can see but which itself is invisible, so the prophet is saying, God's wind, God's breath, God's Spirit (all translating the same words in both Hebrew and Greek), is powerfully if invisibly at work in our world, even as in today's Gospel reading, by a seemingly miraculous act of healing. Healing itself is a good example of God's invisible power at work, for all that we know about healing and for all the advances in neuroscience, there still is a great deal of mystery about the whole healing process that is not fully reducible to scientific, empirical explanation like the "placebo effect," e.g.

Now don't get me wrong. I'm not arguing for a "God-of-the-gaps" view of things, that old-fashioned Christian apologetic that mistakenly finds God only in the empty spaces of human understanding. The problem there, of course, is that the more scientific progress is made and our knowledge of nature expands and deepens, God is increasingly made homeless in our world.

Rather, I believe with Isaiah as a matter of faith and not sight that it is God who "comprehends" all of reality—the whole created order, the cosmos and the chaos that surrounds it—and not that God inhabits only the gaps in our understanding. And the wind—invisible and powerful and life-giving—continues to be a great metaphor for God's "elusive presence" in our everyday world.

"*To whom then will you compare me, or who is my equal?*" God goes on, challenging the people to look around and use their senses to behold God's works in creation. They are plenty visible even though during their time of exile the people feel God's absence more than God's presence within their own "religious experience" and, in effect, taunt God with the dare, "if you're so real and powerful where are you when your people need you?" But yet again God returns rhetorically to those earlier questions that, in effect, challenge Israel's capacity to stand in judgment of the creator of all that is: "*Have you not known? Have you not heard? The Lord is the everlasting God, the Creator of the ends of the earth*" (vv 25–28). "Get over it, grasshoppers," Isaiah's God is saying. The good news is that "You are not God!" but are metaphorically grasshoppers, folks bouncing here and there, sometimes violently swarming our environment like our locust cousins, or sometimes rubbing our legs together to make sounds so others take notice of us, a little like our cousin Jimminy Cricket, wishing upon a star, wondering what or who we are. The good news is that God knows who we are and what we're for, and that the creator of all that exists has somehow managed to shoe-horn the divine presence into the likes of one of us—into an infant born in a cow's manger—in order to make the whole creation's salvation possible. "*Have you not known? Have you not heard?*" You bet you have!

"How Marvelous God's Greatness" (*ELW* #830) sings compellingly of the creation's testimony to God's magnificent creativity as does #837, "Many and Great, O God," sung to a Native American tune.

Sixth Sunday after Epiphany, Lectionary 6

Psalm 30
2 Kings 5:1–14
1 Corinthians 9:24–27
Mark 1:40–45

O Lord my God, I cried to you for help, and you have healed me.
His (God's) anger is but for a moment; his favor for a lifetime.
Weeping may linger for the night, but joy comes with the morning.

—PSALM 30:2, 5

Crossing Boundaries

Robert Frost put the dilemma well in his poem regarding two differently-minded neighbors regarding the wall that divided their properties. "Something there is that doesn't love a wall," he rather memorably if with consciously awkward syntax wrote, noting how walls—especially walls made of rocks—have a tendency over time to fall apart and need continual mending. Something there is that doesn't love the ugly dividing barrier that Israel has erected against its Palestinian neighbors, usurping generations-old, Arab-owned farms and olive orchards in its quest to wall off its justice-seeking as well as angry neighbors. And lest we Americans get too judgmental about all this even now there is an ugly wall continuing to arise on our southern border and even those arguing for one in the north as well. And lest we think this is merely a partisan, political issue, remember President Reagan who while in Berlin once goaded his then still super-power rival, "Tear down this wall, Mr. Gorbachev."

But the other side is given voice by Frost's neighbor who in the poem cites the old adage we know so well: "Good fences make good neighbors." But "why," the poet wonders? We don't have any cows. Before building a wall, he muses, it would only be right to find out what was being walled in or out. But then comes the refrain, "Something there is that doesn't love a wall." But his neighbor responds with his ancestral, contrapuntal refrain, "Good fences make good neighbors," and the poem ends on that unresolved note.[8]

There's been a lot of talk in the church in the last twenty-five years about boundaries, as long hushed-up stories of clergy sexual abuse have been aired and bishops and those in authority have been learning at long last to take allegations of abuse and harassment seriously and put in place policies and procedures that protect the victimized as well as hold responsible the victimizers, including church authorities for trying to avoid scandal by quietly moving the perpetrators to new positions in other places. Attending "boundaries workshops" has become expected for clergy and other professionals.

Today's Gospel story at first sounds much like the exorcism and healing stories that we've been hearing in Mark's Gospel of late. Except this time it's a story about a man with leprosy, which makes it a story about boundaries as well. Leprosy was an umbrella diagnosis in ancient times for many

---

8. Frost, "Mending Wall" 235–236.

sorts of skin disease including what we moderns call "Hansen's Disease" that we were led to think of as leprosy when we were kids—a disease that made one ritually unclean and formally excluded from local community life. I remember seeing in an early medieval stave church in Norway a little slit in the back door of the church through which food for lepers could be slipped out without "contaminating" the benefactor. In fact in the Book of Leviticus, amid all the regulations regarding sex and dietary and other everyday matters, there are fifty-nine verses devoted to how a leprous person is to be treated by the community followed by a chapter of another fifty-seven verses describing the ritual to be followed in restoring a cleansed, formerly leprous person back into community (chapters 13-15). Leviticus 13:45-46, for example, reads: *"The person who has the leprous disease shall wear torn clothes and let the hair of his head be disheveled; and he shall cover his upper lip and cry out, 'Unclean, unclean.' He shall remain unclean as long as he has the disease; he is unclean. He shall live alone; his dwelling shall be outside the camp."*

And so you have the larger context for today's story about Jesus' healing of a man with leprosy, including the interesting detail of Jesus sending the newly-healed, cleansed and purified former leper off with the words, *"go show yourself to the priest, and offer for your cleansing what Moses commanded, as a testimony to them"* (v 44)—precisely what Leviticus chapter 14 describes in excruciating detail as the ritual by which a cleansed leper may be restored to the community. (And, of course, we also have today's long story of the Syrian general Namaan's healing by the prophet Elisha, a story that Jesus will dare to recall in Luke's Gospel as he returns to preach at his hometown synagogue in Nazareth. See too my postil for "Thanksgiving Day, Year A" and its text from Luke 17 of the 10 lepers whom Jesus heals.). But, of course, even more significant is Jesus' boundary-breaking choice to heal the leper as he, *"moved with pity . . . stretched out his hand and touched him"* (v 41). Jesus may have scrupulously acted within the law by sending the healed leper to the priest in order to authorize his complete restoration to community as well as physical health. But Jesus was clearly "out of bounds" by stretching out his hand to touch him. Jesus' decisiveness is even underlined as the words of the leper, *"If you choose, you can make me clean"* become the occasion of his positive, decisive crossing of age-old borders in his ringing declaration, *"I do choose. Be made clean!"*

And, of course, Jesus' inveterate boundary-crossing would become one of the chief marks of his ministry from his healing on the sabbath, to his touching a woman with a flow of blood, from raising the defiled corpse of a little girl to eating and drinking with tax collectors and sinners. Perhaps no single occasion sums it all up as nicely as the story we'll hear near the beginning of the passion story on Palm/Passion Sunday, when, just two days before the Passover, Jesus will find himself in Bethany at the home of Simon the Leper (who knows, perhaps today's nameless leper now made whole and returned to his home and family?). At any rate, here Jesus in doubtful company to begin with, is accosted by a woman with a jar of very costly ointment who beaks it open and pours it over his head—to whose extravagant gesture some object *"in anger"*— perhaps even more in embarrassment— even as Jesus defends her gracious action by asserting that *"she has anointed my body beforehand for its burial."* And what's more, in perhaps the warmest words of commendation he gives anyone in the whole Gospel, Jesus declares, *"Truly I tell you, wherever the good news is proclaimed in the whole world, what she has done will be told in remembrance of her"* (vv 7–9).[9] Jesus the boundary-breaker might just have well have said of the nameless woman, "It takes one to know one." It will be yet another nail in his coffin, the inveterate boundary-crosser in whom God became incarnate, bridging the great divide between divine and human, creator and created.

Yes, I suppose good walls can make good neighbors. But broken-down walls make even better ones. "For something there is that doesn't love a wall." I think it's God! "When Pain of the World Surrounds Us" (*ELW* #704) sings of our need for God's healing to flow through us as does Marty Haugen's popular "Healer of Our Every Ill" (*ELW* #612). "Where Cross the Crowded Ways of Life" (*ELW* #719) is an oldie that sings hauntingly of Jesus' compassion which the *NRSV* here translates problematically as "pity."

---

9. Schussler-Fiorenza has famously used this poignant phrase as the title of her influential "feminist theological reconstruction of Christian origins," *In Memory of Her*.

Year B

Seventh Sunday after Epiphany, Lectionary 7

Psalm 41
Isaiah 43:18–25
2 Corinthians 1:18–22
Mark 2:1–12

*As for me, I said, 'O Lord, be gracious to me;
heal me, for I have sinned against you.'*

—Psalm 41:4

Raising the Roof

The famous last seven words of the church are, as I earlier reported: "We've Never Done It That Way Before!" These are words that no one ever accused Jesus of uttering. But, in fact, it just so happens that there are seven words that close our most peculiar Gospel reading for today that I want to propose as the new "seven last words of the church." I like to think of Mark the Gospel writer smirking as he wrote them, putting words into the mouths of the scribes and the rest of the crowd who had just witnessed Jesus' healing of the paralyzed man who, in memorable fashion, had been let down through the roof of the crowded house in which Jesus was preaching. Seeing the faith of those who had gone to such great extremes, Jesus flummoxed them all by saying, *"Son, your sins are forgiven,"* a seeming nonsequitur to us, perhaps, but to the religious authorities enough to lead them to accuse Jesus of blasphemy, for, as they muttered, *"Who can forgive sins but God alone?"* A good question, to be sure, which Jesus answered by telling the paralytic man lying on the mat in front of him, *"I say to you, stand up, take your mat and go to your home"*—which he promptly did to the amazement of all who glorified God saying, *"We have never seen anything like this!"* (vv 2–5).

These constitute what are the authentic, seven last words of the church, I believe, a spontaneous outburst of astonishment and delight, glorifying

God for the wondrous and surprising thing they had just witnessed and that had left them so non-plussed even as they were still reeling from what they feared had been Jesus' blasphemous claim to be able to exercise God's authority to forgive sin. *"We have never seen anything like this!"* is an authentic response of faith in Jesus, an act of praise, arising out of the new thing that God in Christ by the power of the Spirit is doing in our midst. "We've never done it that way before" is the tired old religious response of those who think they've seen it all, that there's nothing new under the sun, which is an act of bad faith and blasé, irresponsible worship.

It's not new with the church, of course. Our Hebrew scripture reading from Isaiah reminds us that this was a problem for Israel-in-exile as well. I hope you noticed how our reading began, *"Do not remember the former things, or consider the things of old."* If we bother to read back a couple of verses we'll see that the prophet is talking about Israel's exodus from Egypt through the Red Sea, that paradigmatic event of Israel's history and its foundational remembrance which it was charged with not only commemorating but re-living each year at Passover. But here the prophet is saying, so to speak, *"Do not remember the former things, or consider the things of old"*—DELETE! Why? Well, this is why: *"I am about to do a new thing; now it springs forth, do you not perceive it?"* (vv 18–19). And the prophet goes on to confess how tired YHWH has become of Israel's sin, playing the original Jewish comedian by making a kind of joke about how if Israel's offered anything to YHWH over the years as a sacrifice it's been the ever-growing pile of her sin—which, by the way, stinks to high heaven (vv 22–24)!

All of which leads to the conclusion of our Isaiah reading in which YHWH finally gets specific about just what this *"new thing"* is that's about to take place. *"I am,"* YHWH begins in language more than faintly reminiscent of the voice from the burning bush, *"I am the one who blots out your transgressions for my own sake, and I will not remember your sins"* (v 25). The *"new thing"* that YHWH is about to do is to "forget"—to not remember—Israel's sins, but *"to blot out your transgressions for my own sake."* I love that! Not for your sake but for *"my own sake"*—because of who "I am"—the great "I will be who I will be" God, the voice from the burning bush. The liberator God will not be bound by eternal vindictiveness and chooses not to be defined by how high the chosen people have piled up their past transgressions. *"I am about to do a new thing; now it springs forth, do you not perceive it?"*

Jesus was doing a new thing there in that overcrowded house in Capernaum as well—a new thing rooted in God's age-old power to forgive sin which Jesus dared to claim as his own and then transform into the power to create faith and to heal so that everyone in the room was so awe-stricken that they could only glorify God. I imagine such "glorifying" taking the form of something like "God, what just happened!?" as we shake our heads in disbelief and gasp, each in our own way, *"We have never seen anything like this!"*

It reminds me of a story told by the prolific novelist Reynolds Price in a memoir of his struggle with a debilitating spinal cancer that left him a paraplegic. In his book entitled *A Whole New Life*, Price recounts several landmark moments that marked his recovery. He writes of how amid the excruciating pain he faced in his days following surgery and radiation therapy, he awoke one morning to a scene that he swears was not a dream or an hallucination but rather was one of the most vividly real moments he can ever recall. His eyes opened, he claims, to the scene of himself lying on a beach that he immediately recognized to be the shore of Lake Kinnereth, as the Sea of Galilee in Israel/Palestine is now called. A young man with long hair was walking out into the lake, looking back over his shoulder, when he gestured to the reclining Price to get up and follow him into the water. Price recounts how he saw himself get up—he knew it was himself because of the "x" or bullseye that the radiologist had marked on his back. The man walking into the water whom Price now recognized as Jesus looked back again over his shoulder at him and said, "Your sins are forgiven," to which the figure in the scene which Price recognized as himself said, "What about my cancer?" To which Jesus simply replied, "That too."

End of scene, so utterly real to Price that he says he wrote a note about it in the diary he kept at his bedside, a diary not of thoughts but of actual things that had happened each day. From that day, Price testifies, this happening—or whatever we choose to call it, miracle, vision, epiphany, encounter with Jesus, Price insists—marked what he came to see as the beginning of his "whole new life"—a life made whole by his encounter with Jesus which began, to Price, with a word of forgiveness from which his healing commenced.[10] This may sound confusing, to mix matters of forgiveness and healing. But as Paul wrote the Corinthians, *"As surely as God is faithful, our word to you has not been 'Yes and No.' For the Son of God, Jesus Christ . . . was not 'Yes and No'; but in him it is always 'Yes.' For*

---

10. Price, *Whole New Life*, 42.

in him every one of God's promises is a 'Yes' (2 Cor 1:18–20a). (See hymn suggestions for last week.)

Eighth Sunday after Epiphany, Lectionary 8

Psalm 103:1–13, 22
Hosea 2:14–20
2 Corinthians 3:1–6
Mark 2:13–22

The Lord works vindication and justice for all who are oppressed . . .
For as the heavens are high above the earth, so great is his steadfast love
towards those who fear him . . .

—Psalm 103:6, 11

Fresh Wineskins

Eighth Sundays after the Epiphany are not celebrated every year but only in those with extremely late Easters. Today's Gospel reading follows immediately upon last week's and continues Jesus' musing upon the radically "new thing" that God is accomplishing through his ministry of preaching, teaching, healing, and welcome to sinners. The lection begins, in fact, with Jesus' calling of a tax collector named Levi to *"follow me"* while strolling along the lakeside, much as he had earlier called the two sets of brothers who were fisher-folk. Immediately we find him at dinner in Levi's house where *"the scribes and the Pharisees,"* (the official "boundary-keepers" discussed above)*"saw that he was eating with sinners and tax collectors"* and inquire of Jesus' disciples why their master engages in such behavior. Perhaps because he doesn't trust what their answer might be, Jesus, who overhears their question regarding boundaries utters the well known *bon mot* that might well be chosen as the tag-line for his ministry: *"Those who are well* have no need of a physician, but those who are sick; I have come to call not the righteous but sinners" (vv 13–17).

But that's not the only behavioral quirk about which the religious boundary-keepers are curious. People observe that John the Baptizer's disciples and the Pharisees both practice the religious discipline of fasting—but not Jesus' disciples. Why, folks genuinely wonder? Jesus' answer is a stunner and, as usual with Jesus, is not a direct answer but a metaphorical, parabolic one: *"The wedding guests cannot fast while the bridegroom is with them, can they? As long as they have the bridegroom with them, they cannot fast. The days will come when the bridegroom is taken away from them, and then they will fast on that day"* (vv 18–20). It's not that fasting is wrong, Jesus seems to be saying, but it's situationally inappropriate. Behavior suitable to a wedding is celebratory. One doesn't fast at a wedding but feasts in the presence of the bridegroom. Jesus is here sufficiently canny not to directly identify himself as the bridegroom, but the implication is clear. New behaviors are called for.

And then follows what I can't help but hear as one of the clearest examples we have of Jesus functioning as a teacher of wisdom in the sapiential tradition of his people. His choice of near-to-hand, home-spun images will come to mark the simple parables that become such a salient feature of his teaching style of indirect story-telling, beginning, tellingly, with a reference to a matter of normal women's work in the domestic economy of the day: *"No one sews a piece of unshrunk cloth on an old cloak; otherwise, the patch pulls away from it, the new from the old, and a worse tear is made"* (v 21). Would a man of first-century Palestine be expected to know this? I wonder. But certainly Jesus' women hearers would.

But then, perhaps a more widely recognized and even more vivid reference: *"And no one puts new wine into old wineskins; otherwise, the wine will burst the skins, and the wine is lost, and so are the skins; but one puts new wine into fresh wineskins"* (v 22). A piece of common knowledge then, probably, but today not so much. Yet the point is clear: the times are a'changin', as Bob Dylan taught us to say, and the new situation calls for new methods and attitudes because the old simply cannot contain the new that Jesus represents. It's a message in communications that the church has still to learn and that Dietrich Bonhoeffer was struggling with in his prison cell: Can the old wine skins of "religion" be expected to contain the new wine of the Gospel?

The appointed Hebrew scripture reading from Hosea is only one of four *The Revised Common Lectionary* offers over its three-year cycle from this rich but neglected OT prophetic writing. And a look at today's lection (and beyond) offers an insightful look into the way in which YHWH godself was deeply and imaginatively into metaphorical and parabolic teaching long before the time of Jesus. The call to Hosea to marry the prostitute Gomer as a parallel incarnation of God's stormy love affair with Israel, who continued to go whoring after other gods, is a steamy and seamy enfleshing of God's love-relationship with his bride, Israel. (And notice how the "bridegroom" imagery of Jesus' words in today's Gospel picks up this marriage metaphor of old.)[11] Brian Wren's "Great God, Your Love Has Called Us" (*ELW* #358) sings winningly of how "we by love, for love were made."

Transfiguration of Our Lord, Last Sunday after Epiphany

Psalm 50:1–6
2 Kings 2:1–12
2 Corinthians 4:3–6
Mark 9:2–9

The mighty one, God the Lord, speaks and summons the earth
from the rising of the sun to its setting.
Out of Zion, the perfection of beauty, God shines forth.

—Psalm 50:1–2

---

11. See Heschel's *Prophets*, Vol 1, 39–60 as well as the beautiful and singable love song, "What Do You Do When a Promise is Broken?" in *Meet the Prophets*, a cd written and sung by Fr. Montague.

Year B

Translucence

One of my least favorite contemporary hymns that has made its way into our most recent hymnbook is "Shine, Jesus, Shine" (*ELW* # 671), a hymn, I can't help but think, that might've been written by the awe-struck disciple Peter. For, as Mark says, *"he did not know what to say, for they were terrified,"* but garrulous as Peter always was, he still managed to effuse, *"Rabbi, it is good for us to be here."* He then went on to suggest a little building project to memorialize the occasion, as I understand folks over the centuries have found a way to do at nearly all of the traditional sites in Israel connected with Jesus' ministry. Does Jesus really need our encouragement to "Shine, Jesus, Shine?" as if this story is essentially about Jesus' wattage and his power to light up like a blazing Christmas tree "brighter than the sun he glows!" as another hymn boasts?

Instead, we need to see this day of Jesus' transfiguration as the "hinge" in our church year between Christmas and Easter. It's the day in which the Sundays following the Epiphany which have given us time to bask in the warm afterglow of Christmas and its message of what it means for God to have become one of us in this baby Jesus now grown to manhood reaches its climax in Jesus' glorious epiphany on the mountaintop as he appears before his inner circle of disciples in conversation with those two great "shades" of the past, Moses and Elijah, representing Israel's law and prophets.

The Transfiguration is not only the climactic epiphany but is also the hinge on which we turn to the journey to Jerusalem and pivot toward the season of Lent that prepares us for the passion and death of Jesus that looms ahead. What is the significance of Jesus' appearing on the Mount of Transfiguration in the company of Moses and Elijah? I can't help but think that it has to do with the very framing of today's story which begins prosaicly enough: *"Six days later, Jesus took with him Peter and James and John, and led them up a high mountain apart, by themselves"* (9:2). Six days later than what? Well, the immediately preceding verses of the end of chapter eight of Mark's Gospel tell the dramatic story of how Jesus had asked his disciples who people were saying that he was, culminating in Jesus' question *"Who do you say that I am?"* This, of course culminates in Peter's great confession, *"You are the Messiah,"* followed by Jesus' teaching regarding the suffering, rejection and violent death that lies ahead and then, after three days, his rising again. Peter, of course, won't hear it, to which Jesus responds: *"Get behind me Satan!"*—this to the future "pope!" But Jesus isn't done yet. He calls the crowd together and instructs them in his theology of cross-bearing discipleship, concluding with what I think of as the theme-song of his preaching, *"those who want to save their life will lose it, and those who lose their life for my sake, and for the sake of the gospel, will save it"* (Mark 8:31–35). This is the "six days earlier" conversation that prepares the way for the occasion of the transfiguration but particularly Jesus' conversation with Moses and Elijah. While we're not told what they were talking about, it's my hunch that Moses and Elijah as God's sage Word-bearers of old are offering counsel to Jesus as he sets his face to Jerusalem and what lies ahead, even as we, the church, now set our faces toward Jerusalem during the upcoming forty days of Lent. The transfiguration is the pivot point between Christmas and Easter when Jesus once again hears his abba's voice, as at his baptism, sounding from above again declaring reassuringly, *"This is my Son, the beloved,"* but now adding the simple divine directive intended not for Jesus but for his disciples—for you and me—*"Listen to him!"* (v 7).

All the hoopla of Jesus being *"transfigured"* meaning to "be utterly changed" or *"metamorphosized"* in Greek—the same word we use in English to describe a caterpillar becoming a butterfly—accompanied by the *"dazzling white"* imagery that describes light so bright that it alters the way we see things, suggests to me the word "luminescence." Most of us, I suspect, remember from general science class the three distinctions that used to be made regarding the ways in which light appears to us as it encounters different sorts of materials. First, there is "transparency" in which light simply passes through a window in which we say we can see in or out clearly. Hence "obvious," "open," "frank," "candid" are secondary meanings of "transparency." Opposite in meaning is the word "opacity," the adjective being "opaque," which means "not letting light through" as well as "not reflecting light," "not shining or lustrous," and hence, "dull or dark," "hard to understand," or "obscure"—as in a difficult sermon, perhaps!

Distinguished from these two extremes is a third word, "translucent," which comes from a Latin compound word meaning literally to "shine through," not in the same sense as transparency but rather, my dictionary says, "letting light pass but diffusing it so that objects on the other side cannot be distinguished"—like stained glass or frosted windows which many of us are familiar with in our church buildings. I don't want to get overly subtle here but only suggest that "translucence" may be a good metaphor to use in thinking about Jesus on this Transfiguration Sunday, a way that moves beyond the superficial "shine, Jesus, shine" language that hurts our eyes and offends our aesthetic sense. "Translucence" more imaginatively suggests that in Jesus we truly encounter the light of God but in an indirect way that diffuses and refracts the divine glory by passing through the medium of Jesus' human body, becoming a light that we humans can endure, and not only endure but live by, grow toward and in which we aesthetically can revel and glory, enabling and energizing our worship and our work. When I think transfiguration I'm reminded of the beautiful golden-hued rose window of the Strasbourg cathedral or the lovely Chagall stained glass windows of the otherwise aesthetically austere Our Lady's Church in Zurich, stripped of its earlier adornment by the Calvinists. If even the venerable Sarum text, "Oh, Wondrous Image, Vision Fair" (*ELW* #316) with its unfortunate reference to Jesus glowing "brighter than the sun" is a bit garish for you, you might try the far humbler "This Little Light of Mine" (*ELW* #677) which has nothing to do with the Transfiguration of Jesus but a lot to do with our transfiguration through baptism into Jesus! Or how about "I Want to Walk as a Child of the Light" (*ELW* #815)?

SEASON OF LENT

Ash Wednesday
(See Year A)

First Sunday in Lent

Psalm 25:1–10
Genesis 9:8–17
1 Peter 3:18–22
Mark 1:9–15

Good and upright is the Lord; therefore he instructs sinners in the way . . .
All the paths of the Lord are steadfast love and faithfulness,
for those who keep his covenant and decrees.

—Psalm 25:8, 10

Covenant

"The way" or *"the paths of the Lord"* referenced by the psalmist are the promises of God also referred to as God's *"covenant"* and *"decrees."* Promise calls for response and creates response-ability on the part of the people of the covenant, even as in today's reading from Genesis, before the covenant has taken the form of torah in the decrees handed down to Moses at Sinai.

Seven times the word "covenant" (*"berit"* in Hebrew) is found in this passage from Genesis, a word first introduced in 6:18 where God, after instructing Noah to build an ark, declares: *"I will establish my covenant with you . . ."* As the Lutheran OT scholar (and long-time mentor to the campus ministry I served in Ann Arbor), Professor George Mendenhall, pointed out sixty years ago in his influential *Law and Covenant in Israel and the Ancient Near East*, Hebrew scripture's understanding of covenant needs to be seen in the context of the political treaties made between leaders of unequal power in the ancient Near East. Mendenhall's concise definition of covenant is: "a solemn promise made binding by an oath, which may either be a verbal formula or a symbolic action." He goes on: "Such an action or formula is recognized by both parties as the formal act which binds the actor to his promise."[1] Promise lies at the heart of the idea of covenant, and God is always the initiator and the giver-of-one's-word in the successive covenants we'll encounter in our readings throughout this season of Lent. The important point here at the outset is that we recognize that Israel's God is an inveterate promise-maker and promise-keeper in the face of Israel's repeated acts of infidelity and failure to trust God's promises.

In the wake of the flood through which God destroyed all of life because of the earth's corruption and violence, except for Noah and those of his family sheltered in the ark from whom a fresh start was to be made, God says to Noah: *"As for me, I am establishing with you and your descendants after you, and with every living creature that is with you . . . my covenant . . . that never again shall all flesh be cut off by the waters of a flood"* (9:9–11). As we will again encounter in the story of the wilderness wanderings in Lent 4, so here God raises up a symbol of the divine covenant, transforming a symbol of fear and violence (the bow, as in bow and arrow) into the promise of salvation and security. But please note that the rainbow, God's *"sign of the covenant between me and the earth,"* is not, first of all, designed to be a reminder to us of God's covenant/promise. But as YHWH explicitly says, *"When the bow is in the clouds, I will see it and remember the everlasting covenant between God and every living creature of all flesh that is on the earth"* (vv 13–15). You've gotta love that YHWH, don't you, who sets the rainbow in the sky as a sort of string tied around the divine finger, as a reminder of the divine commitment to the covenant promise?

Today's second reading is a peculiar passage excerpted from 1 Peter which includes the perplexing reference to Christ *"who went and made a proclamation to the spirits in prison."* Its selection, I suspect, is due to

---

1. "Covenant" in *Interpreter's Dictionary*, 52. See also, however, Terrien's insistence that covenant be seen in its rich allusiveness to marriage which is widely attested also in Hebrew scripture (*Till the Heart Sings*, 52).

the ensuing reference to the *"days of Noah," "the building of the ark,"* and the *"eight persons saved through water"* (vv 19–20). I've never bothered to count, but the reference is a useful one that recalls the days of typological exegesis for the author goes on to draw a NT analogy to *"baptism, which this prefigured* [which] *now saves you— . . . through the resurrection of Jesus Christ . . . "* (v 21). For Lutherans this will stir a recollection of Luther's "flood prayer" in the baptismal liturgy: "Through the waters of the flood you delivered Noah and his family" (*ELW*, 230). This issues in the irresistible invitation to connect with the covenantal character of baptism which is the form that God's promise takes in the lives of Christians. Noah's covenant is our covenant in Christ through baptism.

The Gospel reading which takes us back to the opening chapter of Mark which, remember, begins with Jesus' baptism in the Jordan by John, describes in the plainest terms of any of the synoptics Jesus' forty-day sojourn in the wilderness into which the Spirit is described as having "driven" Jesus (in comparison to both Matthew's and Luke's "led"). This "compelling" language offers the opportunity to reflect on God's own role in Jesus' temptation and the role of trial and testing throughout God's covenantal history with Israel—as well as in our lives. If you're up to it, take a look at Genesis 22 and the horrible story of the sacrifice of Isaac in light of God's intention to put Abraham "to the test."[2] Don't miss the opportunity to connect this story of Jesus' forty day sojourn in the wilderness to Israel's forty year wandering and the church's forty days of Lent. I'm not much for numerology in itself, but such resonances invite the use of scripture to interpret scripture, what scholars today call "inter-textuality," of which we'll encounter much more as we approach Jesus' passion story.

While I'm no great fan of "thematic" preaching as it often is a temptation to deviate from the churchly discipline of the lectionary, our appointed Hebrew scriptures for Lent this Year B present the opportunity for a series of sermons in which "covenant" reappears as a connecting thread of Israel's story both explicitly and implicitly. Next week we move on to the Abrahamic covenant, next the Mosaic, then the wilderness wanderings, next Jeremiah's declaration of a "new" covenant, all culminating in the passion story itself which includes, of course, Jesus' invocation of the *"blood of the covenant which is poured out for many"* (Mark 14:24) during the last Passover meal he shares with his disciples on the night of his betrayal. Fitting

---

2. See here Levenson's masterly *Death and Resurrection of the Beloved Son* as well as Moberly's *The Bible, Theology and Faith*, 71–161.

hymns include "O Lord, Throughout These Forty Days" *(ELW #319)* or "Tree of Life and Awesome Mystery" *(ELW #334)* which is intended to be sung throughout the Lenten season with special verses added for each week. Best of all is the Latin plainsong chant translated as "O Sun of Justice" *(With One Voice, #659)* which in its third verse sings of how we are "led back again to life's true way," as nice a turn of phrase describing repentance and return to the covenant as we have in hymnody.

Second Sunday in Lent

Psalm 22:23–31
Genesis 17:1–7, 15–16
Romans 4:13–25
Mark 8:31–38

All the ends of the earth shall remember and turn to the Lord;
and all the families of the nations shall worship before him.
For dominion belongs to the Lord and he rules over the nations.

—Psalm 22:27–28

Peter, You Devil!

The words cited above from today's psalmody are the nearly concluding verses of the "righteous sufferer" psalm that we'll hear chanted in its entirety at the conclusion of the Maundy Thursday liturgy during the stripping of the altar and again the next day, Good Friday. Mark's passion story (like Matthew's) itself will find its climax in Jesus' cry of dereliction, *"My God, my God, why have you forsaken me?"* (Psalm 22:1) which are the very opening words of this psalm of lament. Here, the conclusion of the psalm reminds us that even the faithful one's experience of God-abandonment is comprehended within the covenant's assurance of God's steadfast and long-suffering love (see Psalm 139:7–12).

Today's reading from Genesis is one of several accounts of God's deepening and successive promises made to Abram (the first is in 12:1–3, but see also 15:1–6 and 22:15–18) who is here also given a new name, "Abraham." The meaning of the name "Abram" ("exalted ancestor") now is expanded in "Abraham" to become "ancestor of a multitude" in keeping with the references to "multitude" in this giving of the covenant. The word "covenant" appears four times in this abridged passage, which omits reference to circumcision—the sign God makes Abraham and his male descendents to bear as a token of the covenant.

The reading from Romans contains Paul's extended commentary on Abraham as the exemplary one who by faith in God's promise was made righteous apart from the law. The law, of course, was not given until Moses, and circumcision, as we've just heard, was instituted only subsequent to the promise made to Abraham in Genesis 15 (and reiterated in today's reading from the priestly account in chapter 17). For Paul, as we see in vv 20–23, the key verse is Genesis 15:6, "*And he* (Abram) *believed the Lord; and the Lord reckoned it to him as righteousness.*" Clinging in trust to God's promises would become for Martin Luther the definition of faith in light of the new covenant of grace revealed in Jesus Christ.

Our Marcan text narrates Jesus' passion prediction (referred to above in the postil on Transfiguration Sunday), which he couches in third-person "Son of Man" language, his preferred way of referring to himself in Mark's Gospel. Jesus' prophesy of his impending passion and death is denied by Peter, who rebukes Jesus and is in turn rebuked by Jesus in the harsh words, "*Get behind me Satan!*", the Hebrew word meaning "adversary" or "enemy" from the root "to obstruct" or "oppose." Imagine Jesus telling Peter, the future pope, "You Satan, go to hell where you belong," the strongest words we ever hear from Jesus' lips which function as cuss words. "*You're setting your mind not on divine things but earthly things*" (v 33), Jesus explains. Peter thought he was merely scolding Jesus for being so negative and defeatist. "Buck up Jesus," Peter seems to be saying, in the best positive-thinking manner, looking on the bright side of Jesus' messianic potential, from a human stand point. But such a perspective Jesus rejects as satanic.

Funny thing is Peter should've known better, as our first and second readings for today regarding the faithfulness of old Father Abraham witness. As Paul put it, not without a touch of humor: "*He* (Abraham) *did not weaken in faith when he considered his own body, which was already as good as dead, (for he was about a hundred years old) or when he considered the barrenness of Sarah's womb)"* (v 19). In other words, Abraham certainly didn't concede to a merely "human" point of view. But through his God-given faith, what Paul also calls *"hoping against hope"* and what I like to call "hope beyond all hopefullys," Abraham clung to God's promise, absurd as it seemed from a merely human point of view. As Walter Brueggemann has put it:

> But as the story goes, God has more resilience, more confidence in a possible future than does Abraham or Sarah. Then inexplicably this yearned-for, unexpected, desperately wanted baby is born, not of normal human circumstance, but of the power and fidelity of God. This birth is an event-defining explanation, resisting reason. Abraham and Sarah and all of us are thrown back from reason and understanding to the more elemental responses of wonder ... astonishment ... amazement ... gratitude ... praise ... and laughter.

In that moment, Israel had "broken free from all the bonds of reasonable control and technical prediction" and from then on, learned to live "by the inexplicable that evokes gratitude." And so, Brueggemann concludes for all of us who live clinging to God's covenants of old, "We live in a world of surplus surprises that outrun our capacity to control or predict or explain"[3]

It is this "hoping against hope" character of faith to which Jesus is pointing his disciples in his fresh iteration of the promise of old that would become a kind of theme-song of his ministry: *"those who want to save their life will lose it, and those who lose their life for my sake, and for the sake of the gospel, will save it"* (v 35). Or as Brueggemann puts it: "Faith is enacted by those who trust God who imagines well beyond our resistant presuppositions. Such imagination requires a dying and yields utterly new life"[4]. Now that's seeing from beyond a merely human perspective, as Jesus would put it. "Change My Heart, O God" (*ELW* #801) invites us to join in the simple, heart-felt plea for God-given repentance, concluding with the words, "You are the potter; I am the clay,/Mold me and make me; this is what I pray."

---

3. Brueggemann, *Threat of Life*, 4–5, but see also his commentary *Genesis*, 157–162.
4. Ibid., 8.

Postils for Preaching

Third Sunday in Lent

Psalm 19
Exodus 20:1–17
1 Corinthians 1:18–25
John 2:13–22

The law of the Lord is perfect, reviving the soul;
the decrees of the Lord are sure, making wise the simple. . .
More to be desired are they than gold, even much fine gold;
sweeter also than honey, and the drippings of the honeycomb.

—Psalm 19:7, 10

Takin' Care of Business

The church's Lenten trek through the history of our Hebrew forbears in the faith now arrives at Sinai where we hear the Exodus account of YHWH's giving of the law through Moses. The Mosaic covenant, so called, becomes the heart of torah, or Israel's religious constitution as God's people. The exclusivity of God's claim on Israel, *"you shall have no other gods before me"* (v 3), is clearly rooted in God's prevenient liberating action on Israel's behalf: *"I am the Lord your God, who brought you out of the land of Egypt, out of the house of slavery"* (v 2). And so the Mosaic covenant issues in God's self-revelation as a *"jealous"* God who is at the same time a God of *"steadfast love"* (vv 5–6). Then follow the so-called "Ten Commandments."[5]

The second reading consists of Paul's paean to what he calls the *"foolishness of the cross,"* a kind of counter-cultural wisdom song. Nine times the Greek word for wisdom, *"sophia,"* is invoked in these seven verses, words written to a small Greek-speaking congregation located in a commercial and cultural cross-roads where the love of wisdom (*"philosophia"*) could be expected to be almost as great a passion as the love of money. But wisdom

---

5. See Lehman's *The Decalogue* for a reflection on "the meaning of the commandments for making and keeping human life human" as the book's subtitle puts it.

was not only a Hellenistic theme that Paul turned to his own uses to create a hearing for the gospel. It was also an authentic strain within Hebrew scripture as found in such writings as Job, Ecclesiastes, Proverbs and Song of Solomon as well as the Psalms. And, of course, Jesus himself stood in the tradition of wisdom teaching as a spinner of parables and utterer of pithy sayings. Yet here Paul clearly intends to portray the gospel as a kind of anti-conventional wisdom, as a counter-intuitive good news of "*Christ crucified, a stumbling block to Jews and foolishness to Gentiles*" (v 23).

Our lectionary-makers decided that we should hear today not Mark's version of Jesus' expulsion of the money-changers from the temple (11:15–19) which occurs toward the end of his Gospel but from John's Gospel where we encounter it in just its second chapter. This gives us an opportunity to hear the Johannine Jesus' cryptic prediction of his resurrection, which is couched in terms of the temple, which would be destroyed and raised up "*in three days*" (v 19). "*Stop making my Father's house a marketplace!*" (v 16b) is Jesus' stated objection, the Greek translation for "*emporion*," the origin of our old-fashioned word "emporium" in English, or "bazaar" to employ a transliterated Persian word also used in English.

Some years ago at the University of Michigan's campus-wide kick-off lecture for its annual Martin Luther King Jr. Day observance, Professor Cornel West called for our universities to foster in their midst what he called "centers of non-market values" and "fiduciary communities." I couldn't help but think at the time that this was an imaginative way of terming just what our campus ministry aimed to be amid the university in which we found ourself, as well as the church within our larger culture, in a market-driven and market-obsessed age. Even the contemporary church with its well-meaning commitment to outreach and growth is susceptible to adopting marketing strategies and consumer-oriented tactics that are inspired by the conventional "wisdom" of the entrepreneurialism favored in the commercial marketplace. When churches reportedly eschew displaying the cross as a central symbol of our Christian identity (even as decorative crosses proliferate as items of personal jewelry!), Paul's recall of the church to a theology of the cross seems right on target.[6] "*Stop making my Father's house a marketplace!*" is far less a thunderbolt on church bake sales and bingo than it is an indictment of our contemporary consumer-driven cultus that claims the name "church."

---

6. See Hall, *The Cross in Our Context* as well as Forde, *On Being a Theologian of the Cross.*

All this, of course, could be told in light of Exodus 20, in which the ten commandments well up out of the exclusivity of God's covenant claim on this recently liberated clan of ex-slaves now enrolled in God's "wilderness school" as Dan Erlander in *Manna and Mercy* calls Israel's forty-year sojourn in the wilderness. *"You shall have no other gods before me,"* Luther taught us to realize, is not only the first but in a sense the only commandment, since the temptation to let our hearts cling to lesser gods is the mark of our fallen humanity and, especially lesser gods with greater religious appeal as the ensuing story of the golden calf will prove (Exodus 32). The refusal to let God be God, as first told in the story of Adam and Eve in the Garden, is the story of our fundamental sin.

Repeated political efforts to post the ten commandments in our schools and courthouses, not only provide a case study in church-state relations in the US but invite reflection on the civic use of the law, what Luther once called the "*Sachsenspiegel* of the Jews." The disciplining of our life as Christians within our broader civic responsibilities and mutual accountabilities as Americans is an appropriate concern for Lent that may help prevent this season from becoming too inner-directed. Try fostering a discussion group on the Scottish theologian/economist Adam Smith's seminal *Wealth of Nations* from which the idea of the so-called "hidden hand" of the "free market" was popularized. The ELCA's social statement on the economy, "Sufficient, Sustainable Livelihood for All" is a useful resource to help us learn to exercise moral deliberation regarding our American habits of personal consumption that so define our economy. "Canticle of the Turning" (*ELW* #723) sets the sentiments of Mary's "*Magnificat*" to fresh expression, sung to a lively Irish tune.

Year B

Fourth Sunday in Lent

Psalm 107:1–3, 17–22
Numbers 21:4–9
Ephesians 2:1–10
John 3:14–21

> *Some were sick through their sinful ways, and*
> *because of their iniquities endured affliction;*
> *they loathed any kind of food, and they*
> *drew near to the gates of death.*
> *Then they cried to the Lord in their trouble,*
> *and he saved them from their distress;*
> *he sent out his word and healed them, and*
> *delivered them from destruction.*
>
> —Psalm 107:17–20

Snake-Bitten

Here we find John 3:16, what Luther called "the Gospel in miniature," not only set in its larger following context (unlike Lent 2 in Year A when the preceding context including the night-time visit of Nicodemus is narrated). But today we'll also hear the originating story from the time of the wilderness wanderings of Moses and the bronze serpent set on a stick by which the Israelites who had been bitten by serpents could look up and be healed, a story that John sees as prefiguring Jesus' being "*lifted up*" on the cross as the source of our salvation.

The story is a curious one, introduced by yet another occasion of the Israelites grumbling about the primitive conditions of their wilderness sojourn and especially the "*miserable food.*" And so they ask what I learned in logic class to call a "complex question," akin to the proverbial, "when did you stop kicking your dog?" "*Why,*" they ask, "*have you brought us up out of Egypt to die in the wilderness?*" Yahweh's no-nonsense answer is to send snakes—poisonous serpents—that bit the complaining people, which I suppose at least got their minds off the poor food. But many who were bitten died, which led the people to come to Moses repentantly pleading, "*We have sinned against the Lord and against you; pray to the Lord to take the serpents from us*" (vv 5–7). So Moses prayed for the people, to which God responded with the curious command: *"Make a poisonous serpent, and set it on a pole; and everyone who is bitten shall look at it and live"* (vv 8–9). Moses did as he was told and, indeed, it was so, a kind of reversal of the golden calf episode: a graven image becomes the source of healing rather than the object of idolatry—perhaps a kind of divine joke?

The story smacks of what anthropologists might call "sympathetic magic." But for John it provides a prefiguring of how the cross of Christ (think "crucifix" here with the dying Jesus still affixed) provides the miraculous antidote (salvation equals healing in Greek) to humankind's persisting mortal disease called sin which has afflicted us since that first biblical snake story in Genesis 3. Just as God's healing/salvation is made available only through trusting God's Word that the repellent snake on the stick is to be the instrument of healing (itself, of course, an emblem of the very thing that had bitten them), so also the crucified one (equally abhorrent as a reminder of both our human cruelty and our own mortality) becomes by God's promise the instrument of healing/salvation through faith. (See here the provocative writings of the late Rene Girard, who applied "scapegoat" theories to our understanding of Jesus' death on the cross.)

Of all possible stories in the sacred scriptures of his people, this very peculiar tale, John is telling us, is the story that came to Jesus' mind during his rambling conversation with Nick the Pharisee, triggering this most well-known and best-loved articulation of the Gospel of God's love for the world—a love so deep, so profound, so long-suffering, so mysterious, that Jesus could somehow imagine himself in the place of the serpent on a stick, lifted high that all might look on him in their desperation and instead of perishing from the poison of their sin, be healed, and, what's more, inoculated for eternal life with the antitoxin of God's forgiving grace. The peculiar theological genius that lies embedded in the story, of course, is that God is sufficiently canny and creative as to turn the very source of his people's dying into the very thing that would become the source of their healing/salvation.

Today's passage from the (deutero)Pauline writer's letter to the influential church at Ephesus probes even more deeply into the workings of

God's intention to save in language strikingly parallel to John 3:16: *"But God, who is rich in mercy, out of the great love with which [God] loved us even when we were dead through our trespasses, made us alive together with Christ"* (vv 4–5a). In case we didn't get it, the author adds for emphasis, *"by grace you have been saved"* and then, a verse later, goes on to reiterate, in words especially dear to Lutheran ears, *"For by grace you have been saved though faith, and this is not your own doing; it is the gift of God"* (v 8). Even, in Johannine terms, our lifting our eyes of belief to the cross, even our clinging to the promises of God's Word, in Pauline terms, is not our doing but is the *"gift of God"*—*"not the result of works, so that no one may boast"* (v 9).

This covenant of grace culminates in the affirmation: *"For we are what [God] has made us, created in Christ Jesus for good works, which God prepared beforehand to be our way of life"* (v 10). Good works, whether repentance, faith, or love of neighbor, are here to be understood not as our human contribution to or act of cooperation with our salvation but always and only as the *"way of life"* of responsive and responsible living made possible by God's gracious initiative in making us heirs in Christ Jesus to all the covenant promises.[7]

"God Loved the World" (*ELW* #323) sings well our Gospel text while "Jesus, Keep Me Near the Cross" (*ELW* #335) as well as "My Faith Looks Up to Thee" (*ELW* #759) are oldies but goodies that sing truly if sentimentally of the cross as emblematic of our faith.

---

7. See here my essay "Justification in Literature" which uses two Russian short stories to reflect on the convergence between Lutherans and Roman Catholics in understanding the relationship between faith and works as represented in the *Joint Declaration on the Doctrine of Justification* approved by the Vatican and the Lutheran World Federation in 1999.

Fifth Sunday in Lent

Psalm 51:1–12 or Psalm 119:9–16
Jeremiah 31:31–34
Hebrews 5:5–10
John 12:20–33

*Create in me a clean heart, O God, and
put a new and right spirit within me.
Do not cast me away from your presence, and
do not take your holy spirit from me.
Restore to me the joy of your salvation, and
sustain in me a willing heart.*

—Psalm 51:10–12

A New Covenant

The psalmist's plea for a new heart is recast by the reluctant prophet Jeremiah into the forth-telling of a day when the covenant of old (described as God's marriage with unfaithful Israel) will give way to "*a new covenant . . . not like the covenant I made with their ancestors.*" This covenant (the word is used four times), the Lord says, will be one in which torah is put "*within them*" and will be "*written on their hearts*" rather than on tablets of stone as at Sinai.

The promise at the heart of the covenant, however, remains unchanged: "*I will be their God, and they shall be my people*" (vv 31-33). God's declared purpose will be accomplished!

Today's Gospel reading from John 12 depicts Jesus immediately following his triumphal entry into the city (of which we'll hear from Mark next week) to the accompaniment of the hosannas of the crowd and the waving of palm branches. Here he is found prophesying his own death using the typically Johannine figurative language of his being "*lifted up from the earth,*" an act which "*will draw all people to myself*" (v 32).

The earlier verses of this passage from John bear curious resemblance to the synoptics. For example, Jesus' reverie, *"Now my soul is troubled. And what should I say—'Father, save me from this hour?' No it is for this reason that I have come to this hour"* (v 27) sounds remarkably similar to the slightly differing synoptic accounts of Jesus' prayer to his *abba* in the Garden of Gethsemane. Then too his remark, *"Very truly, I tell you, unless a grain of wheat falls into the earth and dies, it remains just a single grain; but if it dies, it bears much fruit"* (v 24), echoes several of Jesus' synoptic parables that employ his favorite image of the seed. So too the punch line, *"Those who love their life lose it, and those who hate their life in this world will keep it for eternal life"* (v 25), is very close to Jesus' characteristic synoptic refrain, *"For those who want to save their life will lose it, and those who lose their life for my sake, and for the sake of the gospel, will save it"* (Mark 8:35, e.g.). For all of John's special theological spin on the Jesus' story, as we approach the extended passion account a convergence with the synoptic passion stories seems evident.

Taken together our appointed texts invite reflection upon God's ever-deepening covenant relationship with Israel culminating in Jeremiah's prophecy of a new covenant. Christians can't help but "overhear" the prophet's Word from God as a promise that will find its fulfillment in Jesus. According to the Hebrews passage, Jesus the *"Son of God"* is also to be understood as a kind of God-appointed eternal high priest. Unlike a priest who officiates *"at the altar of sacrifice,"* however, in words that again are reminiscent of the synoptic account of Jesus in Gethsemane, Hebrews reminds us how *"In the days of his flesh, Jesus offered up prayers and supplication, with loud cries and tears, to the one who was able to save him from death, and he was heard because of his reverent submission"* (5:7). In effect, Jesus the priest becomes the sacrificial offering (overtones of the sacrifice of Isaac in Genesis 22 are strong!) and thereby *"he having been made perfect became the source of eternal salvation for all who obey him"* (v 9).

Both John and Hebrews provide clues as to how Jesus contemplated the end that he sensed lay ahead of him in Jerusalem. Hebrews goes so far as to claim that *"he learned obedience through what he suffered"* and thereby *"having been made perfect"*—might we translate it "completed" or "fulfilled"?—*"he became the source of eternal salvation . . ."* (v 9).

This Lent, Year B, has been a time for the church to be reminded of God's successive covenants—God's promises—of old. Beginning with God's covenant with Noah, we next remembered the covenant with Abraham and

Sarah followed by the covenant given at Sinai and then, last week, the covenant as tested in Israel's forty year "wilderness school." This is the central story-line of scripture, the master-story by which the church continues to live and discover meaning, which finds its OT climax in the new, might we call it "transfigured," covenant announced through the prophet Jeremiah. As Robert Davidson, a former teacher of mine, has put it, "It is Jeremiah's repeated complaint that the obligations of the covenant were ignored by the people. They were happy to bask in all that God had given them, but unwilling to give the obedience which Yahweh expected." Furthermore, it was Jeremiah's "bitter experience," according to Davidson, "that no attempt at reformation, however sincere, could remedy this situation. All broke down on the sheer cussedness of human nature."[8] I love that phrase and can't help but hear it with the Scottish burr of my old Edinburgh professor, "the sheer cussedness of human nature." It's what Jeremiah was referring to in chapter 17 as he lamented, in another famous passage: *"The heart is deceitful above all things, and desperately corrupt; who can understand it?"* (v 9).

The lesson of Israel's successive covenants with God is clearly that between what God expected and what the people gave in response loomed an unbridgeable gulf. As Davidson comments, "Jeremiah knew that this fact"—the sheer cussedness of human nature—"had to be faced or all talk about a new future would end up under the shadow of the same disobedience which had ruined the past. The new covenant passage claims that the unbridgeable can be bridged, but only from God's side." And this is the reason, Davidson concludes, "We can see why the New Testament"—and "Testament" is simply the Latin word for "covenant"—"claims that this hope of Jeremiah's has been fulfilled in Jesus. In him we see the unbridgeable bridged. In him we see a human life which in all its glory and true humanity gives that obedience which Israel was never able to give."[9] In Jesus we behold Jeremiah's "new covenant" not merely announced but embodied—a covenant in his blood we share in week in and week out in our communion together in Christ. Good communion hymns like "Bread of Life From Heaven" (*ELW* #474) or "We Who Once Were Dead" (*ELW* #495) are fitting as well as the Yigdal-based hymn "The God of Abraham Praise" (*ELW* #831).

---

8. *Jeremiah and Lamentations*, Vol. II, 88–90.
9. Ibid., 88, 90.

HOLY WEEK
Sunday of the Passion/Palm Sunday

Mark 11:1–11 or John 12:12–16
Psalm 31:9–16
Isaiah 50:4–9a
Philippians 2:5–11
Mark 14:1–15:47

> *I have passed out of mind like one who is dead;*
> *I have become like a broken vessel.*
> *For I hear the whispering of many—terror all around!*
>   *—as they scheme against me,*
>   *as they plot to take my life.*
>
>   —PSALM 31:12–13

Passionate Irony

Today the church enters upon a week we dare to call "holy." It is a week that, from today's perspective, does not culminate in Easter (the first day of next week) but in the sad silence of the stone-cold tomb in which Jesus' body will be laid at the end of today's Gospel reading. I'm one who appreciates the dual nature of the juxtaposition of Palm and Passion Sunday in a combined liturgical setting. The reading of the Processional Gospel and the entrance rite leading into the sanctuary accompanied by palms and hosannas provide the church with the body language we need to actually experience an "entry" onto the events of Jesus' passion that we will remember in a variety of liturgies throughout the coming week. The congregational reading of the entire passion story, which has become commonplace for many of us, I like to think of as our communal dress rehearsal for the parts we will play in the passion story for the ensuing week.

In the very brief time available for today's sermon which I suggest might better be seen as a prelude to the passion reading (see my remarks on Passion/Palm Sunday, Year A), try to help your hearers to listen for the irony especially evident in Mark's telling of Jesus' passion story. My Webster's defines "irony" as "a method of humorous or sarcastic expression in which the intended meaning of the words used is the direct opposite of their usual sense." Our mock-heroic parade into the sanctuary, palms waving, is itself an ironic action isn't it, maybe a cause for smiles for those passing by on the street and a bit of embarrassment to us participants?

Contrast Jesus' entry into Jerusalem on the back of a donkey, attended by a rag-tag crowd shouting their "hosannas," with the triumphal entry of the Roman governor in his chariot or on his charger accompanied by his legions of troops come to reinforce the Jerusalem garrison during the tension-ridden days of the upcoming Passover week when thousands of the faithful would be flowing into the holy city, and you will sense the irony implicit in Jesus' "alternative" parade which we helped reenact. NT scholar Donald Juel has written:

> Mark's story is deeply ironic, and the irony is bound up with the royal imagery that dominates Mark's narrative of the passion. As readers, we know that Jesus is the Christ . . . The great irony is that it is Jesus' enemies who invest him as king and pay homage. They offer testimony to what the reader knows to be the truth. Of course, Jesus' enemies, whether Jewish or Roman, do not understand in what sense the words they speak are true. Jewish leaders regard the claim to be blasphemous and absurd; Romans view the claim as seditious and outrageous. Nevertheless, they speak the truth—contrary to their intentions and beyond their ability to understand. The irony in the story is pronounced, but it only works if Jesus is the Christ.[1]

Summarizing the irony implicit in the whole Jesus story as narrated by Mark, Juel points out how Jesus "associates with the wrong sorts of people, threatens tradition, and at the climax of his ministry, is executed as

---

1. Juel, *Master of Surprise*, 96–97

a would-be king, rejected by the religious and political authorities, deserted by his followers and abandoned even by God." His ministry simply doesn't fit "established patterns or expectations" and "for precisely this reason, irony," Juel asserts, "is the only suitable means of narrating the climax of the story. Truth is not identical with appearance but must in some way be in tension with it. Jesus is a hero who does not look like a hero." Yet Jesus "must not simply die, but he must die as a King."[2] Find a way to let your congregation in on the artful manner in which Mark is telling us Jesus' story. As always I recommend the lovely but longish hymn, "My Song is Love Unknown" (*ELW* #343) split up throughout the service. I prefer the Welsh tune "Rhosymedre" (*LBW* #94) to that in *ELW* (my grandfather was Hugh Griffith, after all) and ask your organist to play Ralph Vaughan Williams' serene "Prelude on Rhosymedre" for the offertory or postlude.

Maundy Thursday
See Year A

Good Friday
See Year A

Vigil of Easter
See Year A

Resurrection of Our Lord, Easter Day

Psalm 118:1–2, 14–24
Acts 10:34–43 or Isaiah 25:6–9
1 Corinthians 15:1–11 or Acts 10:34–43
Mark 16:1–8 or John 20:1–18

The stone that the builders rejected has become the chief cornerstone.
This is the Lord's doing; it is marvelous in our eyes.
This is the day that the Lord has made; let us rejoice and be glad in it.
—Psalm 118:22–24

---

2. Ibid., 97.

Nothin' To Nobody

The concluding sentence of today's reading from Mark, which is also the final sentence of Mark's entire Gospel, affords a stunning if head-scratching articulation of the Easter good news. *"They said nothing to anyone, for they were afraid"* (v 8b) at first hearing doesn't seem sufficiently good news to merit the fanfare of trumpets and timpani, the promise of which has dragged even infrequent church-goers out of bed this Easter morning. But Mark's Easter Gospel in its very oddity provides the preacher ample opportunity to prevent this crowning festival of the church year from becoming just another rite of spring, transforming it into an occasion for authentic if unexpected and eccentric Gospel proclamation.

Again, see Donald Juel's *A Master of Surprise* (see the citation from Passion/Palm Sunday) for a carefully nuanced and literarily sophisticated interpretation of Mark's surprise ending to his Gospel, which seems to have served as an open invitation to well-meaning ancient faithful to fill in the blanks of the Gospel writer's abrupt and seemingly unfinished sentence which ends with the conjunction "*gar*," meaning "for" or "because." It leaves the reader hanging in mid-air, suggesting, as someone once joked, that it's as if the author of Mark had been dragged off from his writing desk in mid-sentence. Thus arose the so-called "shorter" and "longer" endings appended to the text, as in the *NRSV*, which reflect the early church's dissatisfaction and desire to resolve the unsettling, discordant ending of verse 8 on a superficially more pious and orthodox note by harmonizing with the more conventionally happy endings of the later three canonical Gospels.

I, for one, am grateful that the contemporary church, under scholarly advisement, has resisted the temptation to sanction the more soothing and "edifying" endings, as all too often happens in the final editing of our made-in-Hollywood movies where various endings are field-tested among viewers before the final cut. On Mark's authority, what the women on that first Easter morning experienced at the tomb—really, what encountered them—left them stunned and speechless so that *"they said nothing to anyone."* Allow folks to experience for themselves an uncleaned-up version of the Greek original, which stutters with the crude double negative, "they told nothing to no one"—nothin' to nobody—for they were afraid. The Gospel of the Lord!

Contrarian that I am, I long have been fascinated with Mark's unsettling ending, which seems a good match for our sort of discomfiting, discordant world. For Easter can never be the easily anticipated, naturally expected, outcome of Jesus' passion and death. The resurrection is not just some eternally recurring truth of nature—like the return of the sun and the springtime rebirth of nature in northern climes, like the butterfly bursting forth from the seeming death of the caterpillar's dry cocoon. Such natural images may be as close as we can come to imaging the resurrection. However, they fall dangerously short of the absolutely new thing, the utterly shocking and surprising and even terrifying novelty, that the resurrection of Jesus betokens in Mark's telling of the tale. As Juel suggests in his commentary on Mark, "the surprise for the reader is that the resolution of critical tensions in the story is left for the future." Therefore, "it is only fitting that just as the tomb will not contain Jesus, neither can Mark's story. Jesus is not bound by its ending; he continues into the future God has in store for the creation." In the meantime, Juel concludes, "we can only trust that God will one day finish the story, as God has promised."[3]

Not to be forgotten, of course, is that what stunned the women into silence and fear was the young man in white who encountered them inside Jesus' corpse-less tomb. Beginning with the disarming (if ineffective) words, *"Do not be alarmed,"* and then going on to, *"You are looking for Jesus of Nazareth, who was crucified,"* the young man in white finally gets around to articulating the good news of the gospel: *"He has been raised; he is not here"* (v 6). This too is a needed corrective to the church's penchant for liturgical cheerleading with the oft-repeated mantra "Jesus is risen! Alleluia!" For the authentic good news of Easter is, as the young man in white says, "He has been raised." We need to listen closely to the passive voice of the Easter message. Jesus is not the actor in this matter of resurrection but is the one acted upon.

No less than Peter attests to this crucial fact in today's reading from Acts where he declares in no uncertain terms, *"God raised him on the third day"* (10:40). Or as Paul, in our reading from 1 Corinthians 15 recounts the tradition handed on to him: *"that he* (Christ) . . . *was raised on the third day . . ."* (v 4). God is the actor in the drama of Easter, the very one to whom we heard Jesus crying out into that eerie midday darkness as he hung on the cross, uttering with his last breath, *"Eloi, eloi, lema sabbacthani,"? "My God, my God, why have you forsaken me?"* (Mark 15:34). It is God's raising of Jesus on the first day of the week that is the answer to Jesus' cry of dereliction of Friday—news sufficiently terrorizing and amazing that it initially stunned the women into silence—but not forever, thank God!

3. Juel, *Mark,* 234–235.

Easter hymns, of course, abound in magnificent diversity. I've already presented my case for giving precedence to "We Know that Christ is Raised and Dies No More" (*ELW* #449) which so nicely links the message of Easter with the affirmation of baptism (see postil for Easter, Year A) which I like to follow with the words from Romans found in the opening words of the funeral rite: "*When we were baptized into Christ Jesus, we were baptized into his death. We were buried therefore with him by baptism into death, so that as Christ was raised from the dead by the glory of the Father, we too might live a new life. For if we have been united with him in a death like his, we shall certainly be united with him in a resurrection like his*" (see Romans 6:3–5). For a change, with today's emphasis on the women at the tomb, try the Spanish-language, "Alleluia! Christ is Arisen" (*ELW* #375) which begins, "Run, faithful women, to the graveside."

Second Sunday of Easter

Psalm 133
Acts 4:32–35
1 John 1:1—2:2
John 20:19–31

How very good and pleasant it is when kindred live together in unity!

—Psalm 133:1

Wounded Lord

Robert H. Smith, longtime professor of New Testament at Pacific Lutheran Theological Seminary in Berkeley, left us admirers of his biblical scholarship and pastoral sagacity a posthumous gift edited by his wife and colleague, Donna Duensing. Titled engagingly, *Wounded Lord: Reading John Through the Eyes of Thomas*, I will be using Smith's "Pastoral and Theological Commentary on the Fourth Gospel," as it's subtitled, as a primary resource for our Gospel readings this Easter season, all of which are selected from John's Gospel excepting next week's lection from Luke.

Crucial to Smith's peculiar angle of vision into John's Gospel, as suggested by its title, is today's story of Jesus' post-resurrection encounter with the disciple Thomas who was absent on Easter evening, the text says, when the risen Jesus had first appeared to his disciples. Smith's insight is that in this passage, which may well have been the original conclusion of John's Gospel, Thomas "is not being held up to our scorn . . . as a person of stubborn doubt" bur rather "as a model of deep and impressive discernment . . . as one who asks exactly the right question and then utters the truest confession." "The confession of Thomas, ('My Lord and my God')," Smith asserts, "is the parade example of what has been called John's 'high Christology.'" But, more importantly, Smith insists that "John is using the story of Thomas to declare that Jesus without wounds, and that means a Jesus without a cross, is not adequate to meet the deepest needs of humankind."[4]

For those of us who chafe at John's emphasis on the "exaltation" and "glorification" of Jesus on the cross, fearing a gilding of the cross rather than a grappling with the mystery of Jesus' abasement and sense of God's abandonment in his cruel, criminal's execution as depicted in Matthew and Mark, Smith's perspective rescues John from the charge of articulating a "theology of glory" rather than a genuine "theology of the cross." For, as Smith testifies, "In this story at the climax of John's gospel, I hear Thomas saying loudly and clearly, 'I will not confess as 'my Lord and my God' anyone, even one who has been seen as resurrected and glorified, if that one does not have wounds . . . I will not believe or trust or confess Jesus as prophet or Christ, as Savior of the World or Son of God—even if he has vacated his tomb—unless he has wounds.'" Alternatively, "With this story of Thomas, John is proclaiming that a cross-less Christ, an unwounded Christ, an eternally living but merely powerful Christ, is not the answer." Smith concludes with this pastorally provocative insinuation, rich with post-Easter homiletical possibilities, "Such a Christ might in fact be the problem."[5]

Not only does John's Gospel lend a sense of unity to this Easter season, but also our first readings from the Acts of the Apostles testify to the impact of the message of Easter rippling outward into ever-widening contexts for the mission of the followers of the Way as Jesus' followers will come to call

---

4. Smith, *Wounded Lord*, 5, 4.
5. Ibid., 5.

themselves. The American novelist, Larry Woiwode's book entitled *Acts*, described as "a writer's reflection on the church, writing, and his own life" affords an eccentric opportunity to gather a book study group during the Easter season. Or use Jaroslav Pelikan's equally unusual commentary *Acts*, which is part of a Brazos series of commentaries written with special reference to the Christian dogmatic tradition (Pelikan was one of my teachers and author of a five-volume history of doctrine).

But the season of Easter's second readings are also all drawn from a single source, the First Letter of John which offers yet another perspective on the early church's struggle to maintain the unity of the gospel within the diversities of the early church. Here see the noted Roman Catholic New Testament scholar Raymond E. Brown's studies on the evolving Johannine tradition as seen through both the Gospel and Letters of John in his *The Community of the Beloved Apostle*, aptly if not briefly subtitled, *The Life, Loves, and Hates of an Individual Church in New Testament Times* as well as his *The Gospel and Epistles of John: A Concise Commentary* both of which offer easier entrée to Brown's work than his massive Anchor Bible commentaries on the Gospel and Letters of John. An adult education offering during the Easter season on the First Letter of John and the Johannine communities or the challenging topic of the early church's struggle for unity within diversity as revealed in our Easter texts would be most timely.

For more on the "mysterious case of the missing disciple" and my particular take on where Thomas may have been that first Easter evening see my postil for Easter 2, Year A. Also, for a story of the use of our text from Acts as the basis of an "Invocation" I once delivered to the LA County Board of Supervisors see my reflection "Invoking in Public." "We Walk By Faith and Not By Sight" (*ELW* #635) is a singable hymn inspired by our Gospel reading as is "O Sons and Daughters" (*ELW* #386) which can be split up throughout the service due to its length.

Year B

Third Sunday of Easter

Psalm 4
Acts 3:12–19
1 John 3:1–7
Luke 24:36b–48

There are many who say, 'O that we might see some good!
Let the light of your face shine on us, O Lord!'

—Psalm 4:6

A Ghost Story?

If last week's Gospel reading suggested the genre of detective fiction regarding the case of the missing disciple, Thomas, today's reading from Luke's continuing Easter narrative is something of a ghost tale by the Evangelist's own admission. As with last week's reading from John's Gospel, the risen Jesus greets his followers with a word of "*Shalom*"—"Peace be with you." The effect of his unexpected presence, however, Luke wants us to know, is that "*they were startled and terrified, and thought that they were seeing a ghost*" *(36b–37)*. A ghost, I always can't help but think, whom they well may have feared was sent by God to "haunt" them for their having abandoned their master at the time of his arrest on Thursday evening and for not having shown up at all for his passion and death, save Peter's cowardly denial. What's more, that very same Sunday morning they had rejected out of hand the testimony of the women who had visited Jesus' tomb as nothing more than "*an idle tale*" not to be believed (v 11). According to the story of the risen Jesus' encounter with the two disciples returning to Emmaus, which immediately precedes today's gospel reading, already the women's perplexing Easter testimony was being interpreted and dismissed by the disciples "*as a vision of angels who said that he* (Jesus) *was alive*" (v 23). Had this vision now morphed into a ghost, sent by God to startle and terrify them?

However, as in John's story of Jesus' appearance to the disciples, this is no avenging spirit sent to punish the disciples. It is Jesus himself who begins by acknowledging—if wondering at—their fear by asking a question, as he was so often known to do: *"Why are you frightened and why do doubts arise in your hearts?"* Then, with shades of John 20, Jesus bids them, *"Look at my hands and my feet; see that it is I myself."* Here, too, for Luke the authenticating mark of the risen Jesus' presence is the marks of his wounds, as Robert Smith suggests. Further, as in John, Jesus insists, *"Touch me and see,"* and with, perhaps, a trace of a smile lifting the corner of his mouth, having a little fun at his disciples' expense, *"for a ghost does not have flesh and bones as you see that I have."* As if this were not enough, Luke reports of Jesus, *"and when he had said this, he showed them his hands and his feet"* (vv 38–40).

Yet Luke is not done with his tale of Easter evening and of the disciples' chronic failure to credit the good news of Easter now standing right before them. *"While in their joy they were disbelieving and still wondering,"* Luke begins, nicely describing their continuing befuddlement and confusion of emotions. But next the Gospel writer puts in Jesus' mouth one of the great comic non-sequiturs of all time, worthy of Woody Allen or Mel Brooks: *"Have you anything to eat?"* In effect Jesus is saying, "What do I have to do to get you to trust that I'm really alive—eat a tuna sandwich or a bit of gefilte fish? And so, Luke recounts, *"they gave him a piece of broiled fish, and he took it and ate it in their presence"* (vv 41–43). All of this, of course, is intended as evidence of the resurrected Jesus being no mere ghost.

But that isn't the end of the story. Jesus goes on to hold a kind of Bible study with the disciples squaring what he had taught them while he was with them during his ministry with what he calls *"everything written about me in the law of Moses, the prophets, and the psalms"* which had to be *"fulfilled."* And then, Mark says, in what I find to be a remarkable phrase *"he opened their minds to understand the scriptures"*—everything regarding the suffering of the Messiah, his rising from the dead and the forgiveness of sins that was to be proclaimed to all. And he concluded by saying *"You are witnesses of all these things"* (vv 44–48), words that overflow that first Easter evening to become the co-missioning of the disciples to their calling (and the church after them) as *"martyroi"* to the good news of Jesus Christ, as we find Peter testifying so compellingly in our first reading from Acts. How significant it is that their preparation to be *"martyroi"* to the good news of the gospel involved Jesus' *"opening their minds"* to the true meaning of scripture and how it was to be read in the light of the events of Jesus life, death, and resurrection which they themselves had just experienced without adequately understanding. "Opening minds" in the manner of Jesus is indeed the mission of the church.

But in our Acts passage we also find Peter using an under-appreciated title for Jesus, that I think has the power to reinvigorate our trinitarian God-talk, in which the patronymic "God of Abraham, Isaac and Jacob"—aka, the "God of our ancestors"—is now seen as refracted through the human prism of Jesus who is to be worshipped and served and witnessed to, Peter suggests, as the "Author of Life." "Life's Author" is surely resonant with echoes of Genesis 1, John 1, and last week's second reading from 1 John 1, highlighting the originating creativity of the one whom God raised from the dead, through whom, according to the prologue to John's Gospel, *"all things came into being"* and in whom *"what has come into being was life, and the life was the light of all people"* (John 1:3–4). To be "martyrs of Easter" is to "practice resurrection," in the provocative phrase of the farmer-poet, Wendell Berry, which begins by defying all death-dealing, anti-life forces in the world on behalf of the Author of Life. This certainly includes the mandate to cherish the earth and all its creatures, as the church joins with others in celebrating this month on Earth Day. The contemporary hymn "Touch the Earth Lightly" (*ELW #739*) nicely expresses the earth-keeping dimension of God's authorizing call to care for creation with as much God-given imagination and ingenuity as we can muster amid a political culture that is largely in denial. See too Terence Malick's stunning film, "The Tree of Life," for further inspiration in relating the details of our individual human stories to the story of the Author of Life.

Fourth Sunday of Easter

Psalm 23
Acts 4:5–12
1 John 3:16–24
John 10:11–18

The Lord is my shepherd . . .

—PSALM 23:1A

Shepherding

This Fourth Sunday of Easter is known as "Good Shepherd Sunday" since every year the appointed Gospel reading is one of three passages from Jesus' long and rambling discourse in the tenth chapter of John in which he expounds on what it means for him to declare, *"I am the good shepherd."* This language is so familiar to us in the church that it is easy to miss the utterly radical implications of Jesus claiming for himself this title. For, as Robert Smith puts it, "shepherding is a political term" that speaks of "kingship" or "generalship" (see, e.g., Jeremiah 3:15, 10:21, 23:1–4, and Ezekiel 34:1–10, 37:24).[6]

However, "good shepherd" is also God-language in the Hebrew Bible, one of the more frequent metaphors for God used in scripture. To find Jesus invoking this title for himself is blasphemous from a traditional point of view, which he escalates later in John 10 to the audacious claim that *"the Father and I are one"* (v 30)—which, not surprisingly, leads his outraged hearers to take up stones intending to kill him.

Smith asserts that "the cross," according to John's theology, "is the ladder by which Jesus ascends to his rightful place of leadership over the flock" while "others try to climb up to leadership 'by another way,' any way but the way of the cross." Such others, whom Jesus calls *"strangers,"* seek to "avoid the cross because they seek a different kind of glory and they wish to exercise a different kind of leadership." Further, "Jesus does not deplore his death or describe it as the work of his enemies. In fact, he gives no hint that others rip his life from him." Instead as in v 15 and following he simply, if solemnly, says, *"I lay down my life for the sheep,"* which he does quite deliberately, Smith claims, in his own memorable phrase, "in an act of magisterial freedom."[7].

Not to be ignored is the strikingly similar language of today's second reading from the First Letter of John, in which Jesus' language of John 10 (including even the same Greek verb for *"lay down"*) is clearly echoed in the affirmation, *"We know love by this, that Jesus Christ laid down his life for us."* This then becomes the gospel mandate that *"we ought to lay down our lives for one another."* Jesus' cross empowers the agapaic, self-giving behavior that alone is able to answer the age-old ethical question that confronts us all: *"How does God's love abide in anyone who has the world's goods and*

---

6 Smith, *Wounded Lord*, 98.

7. Ibid., 99, 101.

sees a brother or sister in need and yet refuses to help?" The answer never can be merely rhetorical, as the Letter's author insists, but must be real and practical for *"love"* is a matter not of *"word and speech"* but of *"truth and action"* (vv 16–18).

"It is a tradition of long standing," Smith asserts, "to interpret the evangelist as saying that 'Jesus is like God.'" But we come closer to John's teaching "when we think of him as saying that 'God is like Jesus'" [8]—the invisible Word of God enfleshed and bloodied in self-giving love.

Today's readings authorize an orgy of ovine overkill (see the postil for Easter 4, Year A). Have your organist perform Bach's "Sheep May Safely Graze," or play a CD of the Jacques Loussier Trio's jazz version if you are bereft of a musician capable of playing it. Today's 23rd Psalm invites special attention as nearly everyone's favorite. I remember my non-church-going Welsh grandfather bribing me as a boy to learn it "by heart." Explore why it is so popular in your sermon, children's sermon or adult class. Exploit the profusion of musical versions available in our hymnody, contemporary and traditional, as well as choral settings. The fact that Lutherans in North America long ago opted for "pastor" (Middle English for "shepherd") as our preferred title for clergy invites pondering how shepherd and sheep imagery might enliven our imaginations around issues of servant leadership in the church.

A particular claim that Jesus as good shepherd makes in today's reading may strike us as especially good news. It corrects a misunderstanding of Peter's words about Jesus in our second reading from Acts where he says, *"There is salvation in no one else for there is no other name under heaven given among mortals by which we must be saved"* (Acts 4:12). "Non salus extra ecclesiam" is the Latin phrase meaning "there is no salvation outside the church" that imperial Christendom would in time arrogate to itself as the church's monopoly on God's salvation. However, Jesus' words in John 10 pre-empt such an exclusivistic reading, as he declares in v 16, *"I have other sheep that do not belong to this fold. I must bring them also, and they will listen to my voice."* He concludes in what we today might well hear as universalistic, non-imperialistic language, *"So there will be one flock, one shepherd."* Which is all the more reason for us to work at finding a way to use these readings to help proclaim a gospel that unifies rather than divides our contemporary flock of believers, for whom appreciation for multicultural and multi-faith realities is continually threatened by growing political

---

8. Ibid., 105.

divisiveness and xenophobia in our "nation of immigrants" and our global reality of the crisis of refugee and migrating peoples.

Fifth Sunday of Easter

Psalm 22:25–31
Acts 8:26–40
1 John 4:7–21
John 15:1–8

> *... future generations will be told about the Lord,*
> *and proclaim his deliverance to a people yet unborn ...*
>
> —PSALM 22:30B–31A

What is to Prevent?

Our first readings throughout this Easter season have all been taken from the Acts of the Apostles, volume two of Luke's writings. We have been led through a continuing series of stories in which the Spirit of God is depicted as wafting our earliest Christian forbears into ever new situations, presenting them with ever more challenging opportunities to proclaim and practice the gospel in circumstances increasingly remote from the old orthodoxy centered in Jerusalem.

In today's reading, the Spirit gusts the mission of the early church toward new frontiers of the gospel on a number of fronts, geographically, racially and sexually. The story is one of the most charming and exotic in all of scripture. As do so many of Luke's stories, it begins with an angel, a messenger of God, directing Philip to *"get up and go toward the south to the road that goes down from Jerusalem to Gaza"* (v 26). Our attention immediately is engaged because Gaza is a place of no little contemporary significance.

The text says simply that Philip *"got up and went,"* no ifs, ands, or buts. What did Philip find on this remote desert road on the way to Egypt? Here

Luke painstakingly describes the scene, piling up one adjectival phrase on another. For what encountered Philip was *"an Ethiopian eunuch, a court official of the Candace, queen of the Ethiopians, in charge of her entire treasury"* who had *"come to Jerusalem to worship and was returning home."* And, perhaps, most oddly, *"seated in his chariot, he was reading the prophet Isaiah"* (vv 27–28). Luke uses seven highly descriptive phrases to engage our curiosity and set the scene whose action is initiated by Philip's condescending query, *"Do you know what you are reading?"* To which the man replies without taking offense: *"How can I, unless someone guides me?"* (v 31). This turns out to be just the opening Philip is looking for to join the man in his chariot and read with him the scroll of the prophet, while proclaiming the *"good news about Jesus."* A pretty bizarre scene for the occasional camel driver passing by, I can't help but think, though maybe no stranger than the sight of Philip dunking the man in a nearby pool of water in response to the man's query, *"What is to prevent me from being baptized?"* "Nothing is to prevent" is Philip's unspoken answer after which the man *"went on his way rejoicing"* (vv 34–38), as we join in singing the old hymn (*ELW* #537).

It is a wonderful story, literally a story at which to wonder. But I find it particularly wondrous that having introduced us to this exotic person with such careful description it is the man's sexual condition as a eunuch by which Luke chooses to identify the man subsequently four times—a person formally excluded from the worshipping community of Israel according to Deut 23:1. What's more, Luke tells us that the eunuch is reading chapter 53 of Isaiah, just a short turn of the scroll earlier than chapter 56 where the prophet shockingly reverses torah's exclusion of eunuchs and explicitly welcomes them into the covenant community *"with a name better than sons and daughters . . . an everlasting name that will not be cut off"* (56:5). Ouch! Pun, I expect, intended.

The welcome of eunuchs into the faith community is not the issue on the frontier of the church's mission with sexual minorities of our day. But we know what is. *"What is to prevent?"*, the eunuch's question, becomes the Spirit's encouragement to extend and include the welcome of the gospel and the offer of baptism into the Way of Jesus to all, including, as we'll see in next week's reading from Acts 10, even uncircumcised gentiles—the likes of most of us (at least the "gentile" part).[9] Acts is honest in portraying for us the challenges, discomfort, and resistance that some among the early church, including its leaders, evinced in the midst of these ever-ex-

---

9. For a text of this entire sermon see Ericson's *Rhetoric of the Pulpit*, 91–98.

panding liminal situations into which they were continually being drawn. Nevertheless, Luke wants us to be reassured that it is the gusting Spirit of God that is blowing the church beyond the covenant community's familiar boundaries.

Both today's Gospel from John 15 and second reading from 1 John 4 are one in describing the gracious gift of "letting go and letting God" as together they no less than fifteen(!) times employ the same Greek verb "*meno*" that is usually translated into English as "abide" but that also carries the connotations of "remain," "stay," "live," "last," "endure," and "continue." I like the colloquial phrase "hang in there" or the fussier "perdure." The point of the word, like Jesus' image of the vine and the branches in John 15, is that our imperative is to "stay connected," to not opt out or try to go our own way but as 1 John 4 makes clear, to abide in love—to hang in there even as God hangs in there with us.

This was the word that the Johannine community within the early church especially needed to hear and trust, precisely because of its own sectarian tendencies and desire to be a church of "true believers."[10] And it's surely a word the church of our day needs to hear and heed as the Spirit continues to waft us onto ever new frontiers of mission. Today would be a good day to sing Marty Haugen's thrilling "All Are Welcome" (*ELW* #641).

Sixth Sunday of Easter

Psalm 98
Acts 10:44–48
1 John 5:1–6
John 15:9–17

*O sing to the Lord a new song, for he has done marvelous things.
All the ends of the earth have seen the victory of our God.*

—Psalm 98:1, 3b

---

10. See Brown's earlier mentioned *Community of the Beloved Disciple*, 103–144.

Year B

Friends

From "Cheers" to "Seinfeld" to the eponymously named "Friends," television sitcoms often rely on the tried and true format of providing the viewer vicarious access to a tightly bound network of friends to which we become attached. Facebook, Twitter, and other social media are carrying such "friending" to yet another dimension, whether virtual or real, whether for good or ill, who knows? Yet we seem to have an insatiable longing to have access to that utopian community "where everybody knows your name," as the old "Cheers" theme-song put it.

It's less common to think about friendship in terms of our faith. In the church, we are much more familiar with "love" talk. By my count today's readings from 1 John and John's Gospel use the word "love" a total of fourteen times! Many of us are aware that in Greek there are three different words that are all translated as "love" in English. The first, *"eros,"* is the root from which our word "erotic" derives. It is a word that can mean passionate love, the kind of love that desires the other for itself and can lead to a kind of out of control intoxication—love bordering on lust, which the word "eroticism" connotes. This very common Greek word, interestingly, never appears in the NT.

The second Greek word for love is *"philia,"* which can be translated as friendship or devotion or even affection. We easily think of words like "philosophy," meaning love of wisdom, or "philanthropy" meaning love of humanity or the strong NT word *"philoxenia"* literally meaning love of the stranger which we normally translate as hospitality. But *"philia"* can also mean something as simple as a kiss, a sign of physical affection.

Finally, the Greek word *"agape"* is the word most frequently translated as love in the NT. *"Agape"* is love in the strong, and almost untranslatable sense, of Christian love—love in its fullest sense as we encounter Jesus commanding *"love your enemies"* in Matt (6:44) or as in today's reading from John's Gospel where Jesus tells his disciples of God's love for him and for them, and then commands them to bear the fruit of love in their lives (vv 9–16). *"God is love"* (v 8b) we heard in last week's reading from 1 John 4, leading on to the exhortation, *"Beloved, since God loved us so much, we also ought to love one another"* (v 11).

In today's reading from John's Gospel we hear Jesus saying, reminiscent of our readings a couple of weeks ago, *"No one has greater love (agape) that this, to lay down one's life for one's friends (philoi)."* Jesus goes on to describe his disciples as *"philoi"* twice more in the following verses: *"You are my friends (philoi) if you do what I command you. I do not call you servants any longer, because the servant does not know what the master is doing; but I have called you friends (philoi), because I have made known to you everything that I have heard from my Father. You did not choose me but I chose you"* (vv 14–16).

I have a friend, a former colleague in campus ministry by the name of Don Postema, who first helped me to see the depths of what Jesus was trying to get us all to see by using three times this word "*philoi*" in the midst of his more characteristic "*agape*" talk. I remember Don insisting that too many of us Christians suffer from a kind of "arrested development" of the faith that fixates us into viewing ourselves as perpetual children in our relationship to our fathering/mothering God. What Don argued was that by elevating us from the status of children and slaves or servants to the status of friends, Jesus in effect is welcoming us into a mature faith relationship, akin to that of an adult child's relationship to one's parent(s). At its best, this is a relationship no longer of mere dependency, inferiority, or childishness in either its reactionary/obedient or adolescent/rebellious modes. Instead, a mature relationship exists in which the parent is still parent but whose love for the child is expansive and liberating rather than merely protective and directive, as may once have been appropriate and necessary.[11]

Is it too much to hope that the church itself as Jesus' continuing band of disciples might profit from adding the metaphor of friendship to its various "models of the church," as Avery Dulles once termed them? At least it provides an alternative to the too often cloying metaphors for church as "family," or worse, "family system," which seem to dominate our practical theology.[12] The oldie but goodie "What a Friend We Have in Jesus" (*ELW* #742) is about the only hymn that readily comes to mind. Hymnodists get busy!

---

11. Postema, *Catch Your Breath*, 62–67.
12. Dulles, *Models of the Church*. See too Meilander, *Friendship*.

Year B

Ascension of Our Lord
(See Ascension of our Lord, Year A)

Seventh Sunday of Easter

Psalm 1
Acts 1:15–17, 21–26
1 John 5:9–13
John 17:6–19

*They are like trees planted by streams of water,
which yield their fruit in its season, and their leaves do not wither.*

—Psalm 1:3a

Martyrs

On Thursday last when the church celebrates (or more often, declines to celebrate) the Ascension of our Lord, we heard Jesus bid farewell to his disciples (followers), now commissioned to be apostles (sent-out ones) by promising them the Holy Spirit who would empower them to be "witnesses" (Luke 24:48). This word *"martyres,"* as well as its congnates in Greek, is familiar to us English-speakers through its transliteration as "martyrs," commonly meaning those who suffer death rather than give up their beliefs or principles. The history of the church under the Roman Empire prior to Constantine is full of stories of those who gave their lives rather than recant their faith in Jesus Christ, the likes of Polycarp and Justin and Ignatius, of Perpetua and Felicity and many more. Others, like Stephen and the apostles Peter and Paul, as well as nearer contemporaries like Dietrich Bonhoeffer, Martin Luther King, Jr. and Oscar Romero are appropriately thought of as martyrs as well.

The word "martyr" does not appear in today's Gospel reading from John 17, which nonetheless contains Jesus' prayer that God protect his followers from the *"evil one"* (v 15) even as he is about to send them into a world that he prophesies will hate them because *"they do not belong to the world*" (v 14). These disciples, whom we heard Jesus call *"friends"* a couple of chapters back, he prays to his abba, are those who *"have kept your word . . . for the words that you gave to me I have given to them, and they have received them and know in truth that I came from you"* (vv 7–8). "Truth" here stands for the witness (*martyros*) entrusted by God through Jesus to his followers. Jesus adds, *"As you have sent me into the world, so I have sent them into the world"* (v 18). These words function for John's Gospel as equivalents to Jesus' great commission in Matt 28:19–20 and his promise of Pentecost in Acts 1:8. Further, they constitute the rationale for the need to select a replacement for Judas that we learn of in today's first reading from Acts 1:25. A criterion for this replacement was that it be one *"who accompanied us during all the time that the Lord Jesus went in and out among us"* who *"must become a witness (martyra) with us to his resurrection"* (vv 21–22).

It's in today's second reading from the ultimate chapter of 1 John, that we find ourselves awash in martyr language. Seven times in five short verses the Greek word "martyr" or its cognates encounter us here in the *NRSV* which translates them as *"testimony"* or *"testified."* Rhetorically we are bathed in martyr talk, a testimony that those who believe in the Son of God bear in their hearts. So what is this "martyr," this "witness," this "testimony?" First John introduces it with what I can't help but hear as a fanfare of trumpets—ta da!: *"And this is the testimony: God gave us eternal life, and this life is in his Son"* (v 11). This, in a Johannine nutshell, is the gospel—the testimony—the witness to which we are called to be martyrs with our lives, even to the death when need be. This is our Easter calling, to be martyrs to the resurrection of Jesus, God's promised inheritance of life that death cannot hold.

Years ago one of the congregations I served as pastor was about to celebrate a significant anniversary and decided that this milestone would be a good occasion to adopt a new mission statement. The mission objectives and commitments were well stated and comprehensive if a bit prolix. What made the statement memorable and a bit edgy, however, was the final sentence, which was intended to make sure that people would pay attention to what they were committing themselves in the statement: "We live, willing to die, for the sake of these commitments." We were committing ourselves, at least rhetorically, to being martyrs.

Robert Smith has again put it vividly in his commentary on our Gospel reading: "Jesus is the outward and downward movement of God, sweeping through a dark and unbelieving cosmos. He descends to speak the truth of

God with every breath and deed, and he mounts up to God again by means of the ladder of the cross. In that coming down and going up again he calls and gathers people into his own upward motion, up from darkness and lostness, up from unknowing and unbelief into the life of God."[13]

Now and again, I have found myself resorting to a piece of ancient Christian literature as eloquent and compelling testimony to the martyr or witness of early Christians to the empire of their day. The Epistle to Diognetus, dated about 200 C.E., is worth mining for your congregation's inspiration. Here are a few nuggets:

> Christians are not distinguished from the rest of mankind by either country, speech, or customs . . . While they dwell in both Greek and non-Greek cities, as each one's lot was cast, and conform to the customs of the country in dress, food, and mode of life in general, the whole tenor of their way of living stamps it as worthy of admiration and admittedly extraordinary . . . Every foreign land is their home, and every home a foreign land. They marry like all others and beget children; but they do not expose their offspring . . . They spend their days on earth, but hold citizenship in heaven. They obey the established laws, but in their private lives they rise above the laws. They love all men, but are persecuted by all . . . They are poor, and enrich many . . . They are dishonored, and in their dishonor find their glory . . . Doing good, they are penalized as evildoers . . . In a word: what the soul is to the body, that the Christians are in the world.[14]

Now that's a martyr! "Rejoice, Ye Pure in Heart!"(*ELW* #s 873 and 874) is a fitting festal hymn rejoicing in the witness of the martyrs but also try the simple Tanzanian, call and response song "We Have Seen the Lord" (*ELW* #869).

---

13. Smith, *Wounded Lord*, 157
14. In *Readings in Church History*, Vol. 1, ed. by Barry, 151–152.

The Day of Pentecost

Psalm 104:24–34, 35b
Acts 2:1–21 or Ezekiel 37:1–14
Romans 8:22–27 or Acts 2:1–21
John 15:26–27; 16:4b–15

O Lord, how manifold are your works! In wisdom
you have made them all ...
When you send forth your spirit, they are created.

—PSALM 104:24A, 30A

Second Wind

Truth be told we heard as much of the Pentecost story as St. John the Evangelist has to tell back on the Second Sunday of Easter when on that first Easter evening the risen Jesus appeared to his fearful disciples (save Thomas), *"breathed on them and said to them, 'Receive the Holy Spirit'"* (John 20:22). Except in the Greek "Holy Spirit" is not preceded by the definite article and could just as well be translated more literally as "receive holy breath," another connotation, as I've mentioned before, of both the Greek word "*pneuma*" and its Hebrew equivalent "*ru'ah*" which can also mean "wind." I like that Johannine image of Jesus resuscitating the faith of his dispirited followers by breathing resurrection life, "respirating" them, let's call it, empowering them even as he "apostles" them with the words, *"As the Father has sent me, so I send you"* (v 21). John brings the Easter season full circle by returning us to the upper room for his brief story of Jesus' promising of the sending of the Advocate.

The alternative first reading from Ezekiel 37 prefigures the metaphor of respiration for the meaning of Pentecost by its detailing of the prophet's macabre vision of a valley of dry bones reconstituted replete with sinews, flesh and skin by the power of God's Word but only truly revivified by the resuscitating breath (*ru'ah*) summoned by God from the four winds (also *ruah*). Echoes of Genesis 1:2, which speaks of the *ruah* of God sweeping over the face of the waters at creation, and Genesis 2:7, where God is depicted as having "*breathed into his* (the "earthling's") *nostrils the breath of life, and the man became a living being*" reverberate with intertextual allusiveness.

I've never fancied myself a runner, though I can still move tolerably well on the tennis court in short sprints. But I admire—if not quite understand—the stamina of those who can manage to finish longer footraces, and especially marathons. We've all, I expect, heard marathoners describe how at a certain point in the race, they sometimes "hit the wall"—a kind of psychosomatic barrier that at first seems insurmountable, leading them to question their own powers of endurance. Those who somehow find the grit and energy to "run through the wall" often speak of getting their "second wind"—of "catching their breath" as we say. Brad Braxton, NT scholar and pastor, has suggested that Pentecost might well be thought of as the festival of the church's getting its "second wind" from God, the "first wind" being that in-breathing—literally that "in-spiration"—described in the second Genesis creation account mentioned above. Our "second wind" is the Spirit of God, promised by Jesus as our "paraclete" or "advocate," sent at Pentecost and bestowed upon us at our baptisms.[15]

As the Lutheran theologian Gordon Lathrop has explained further, this gift of the Spirit as our "advocate" is simply "God present,"—the present tense of God—"seeing to it that the words and actions of Jesus Christ are alive in our midst as powerful words and actions, judging and forgiving, sending, giving life. The Spirit is all that belongs to Christ, all that pertains to him—and thus all that truly pertains to the ancient God—alive here and declared to us." And so, in terms of last week's Gospel (see above), it is the Spirit that enables the church's "witness"—*martyros*—giving even the likes of you and me sufficient "power that the words about Jesus Christ might be heard universally, that the particular story of a Judean execution might be everywhere life-giving." The Spirit's advocacy inspires us with a second wind to fresh understandings of our calling as church to be, in Lathrop's words, a "free space in the world . . . devoted to the death-reversing judgment of God, for the sake of the life and freedom of the world."[16]

One last thing. Jesus also calls this "paraclete" or "advocate" he promises to send in his physical absence the "*Spirit of truth*" who will "*guide you*

---

15. Braxton, *Preaching Paul*, 125–132.
16. Lathrop, *New Proclamation*, 70–71.

into all the truth" (v 13a). I love that depiction of the Spirit as "truth-teller" because it encourages us in our calling to be truth-tellers, to tell it "like it really is," as Brother Martin used to put it, sticking to a realistic and plain-spoken theology of the cross rather than the fancy-dress clothes of a glitzy theology of glory, which only tells us what we want to hear. Truth-telling is to be a mark of our life together in the church and as church, "*speaking the truth in love,*" as Ephesians puts it (4:15), which means truth-telling as a "body-building" exercise, the opposite of the "truthiness" or phony, mean-spirited "honesty" that marks so much of our current political landscape, as Stephen Colbert has termed it so mockingly. Our God-given Advocate, the Spirit given at Pentecost, both gives us a "second wind" and stiffens our spines so as to be the "martyrs" to the Gospel God calls us to be. As one of our more contemporary Pentecost hymns sings: "Spirit, Spirit of gentleness,/Blow through the wilderness, calling and free;/Spirit, Spirit of restlessness,/Stir me from placidness, wind, wind on the sea;/ You call from tomorrow,/You break ancient schemes./From the bondage of sorrow/All the captives dream dream;/Our women see visions,/Our men clear their eyes./With bold new decisions your people arise" (*ELW* #396)

TIME AFTER PENTECOST, YEAR B
Holy Trinity Sunday, First Sunday after Pentecost

Psalm 29
Isaiah 6:1–8
Romans 8:12–17
John 3:1–17

Ascribe to the Lord, O heavenly beings,
ascribe to the Lord glory and strength.
Ascribe to the Lord the glory of his name;
worship the Lord in holy splendor.

—PSALM 29:1–2

Beyond Two Men and a Bird

Once a year we Christians find ourselves gathered to celebrate explicitly what we mostly take for granted the rest of the year: the identity of God as the three-in-one, Father, Son and Holy Spirit, or, as we say, the "Holy Trinity." I've sometimes used this occasion to focus on how this day is far more than an opportunity to hack away at the mystery of God's triunity, using tried and true analogies like the three-fold character of water (liquid, ice and steam), three forms but at the same time chemically one substance, H2O. I've made fun of traditionally hyper-orthodox accounts that insist on "Father, Son and Holy Spirit" as the formal "name" of God, an almost magical kind of incantation that some insist be used invariably as the words into which we must be baptized (ignoring examples of baptism into the simple name of Jesus). I personally prefer and utilize the so-called "trinitarian formula" in baptism but regret the inference that only these exact words used in "naming God" somehow validate the washing.

This has led me to often take up the neuralgic issue of God-language as a fitting topic, insisting that the Holy Trinity is something more than the patriarchal "two men and a bird" straightjacket that some insist upon, as though "Father, Son and Holy Spirit" is a name for God like all other names, implying that the Holy Trinity is a name just like mine with a corresponding social security number and driver's license as well. For me this is a critical blinding of ourselves to God's utter refusal to take a "name" in the revelation to Moses in the burning bush when the God of Abraham, Isaac and Jacob "revealed" godself to Moses. In effect, to Moses' pleading for a name by which to be able to identify the voice to the folks back in Egyptian slavery, God took the anti-name of "YHWH," saying, in effect, call me "I AM WHO I AM," or as some translate, "I'LL BE WHO I'LL BE." From the burning bush the voice of God declares its independence from all conventional naming, wherein knowing someone's name was thought to give one power over the other. And so, with scripture itself, Holy Trinity Sunday should be a day when we revel in the three-in-oneness of God that obliterates our efforts to name and thereby confine God to our naming but also encourages the disciplined use of our imaginations in discovering apt metaphors and images in describing God in relationship to us humans whom God has invited to be "created co-creators," as Philip Hefner has suggested.[1]

More helpful, however, have been my and others' efforts to honor Holy Trinity Sunday by suggesting and demonstrating how God as triunity has been experienced both in my own life of faith and in that of the larger church. Sometimes, for example, when the rite of confirmation has fallen on this day I've resorted to a story sermon involving details from my own autobiography that bear witness to how I have experienced God as Father, Son and Holy Spirit well prior to my ever consciously reflecting on the trinitarian nature of God—that is, how God as three-in-one in our doctrine is subsequent to our own experience of God and then reflection upon it. Remember the old adage regarding how the dogma of the church is better sung than said. Therefore the liturgy of the church itself as well as its hymns

---

1. Hefner, *Human Factor*, 23–51; see also Wren's, *What Language Shall I Borrow?* for reflections on our use of God-language.

are a great source for reflection as we begin in actual praise and worship of our triune God.

In a little book written well over half a century ago based on a series of radio programs he had done, C. S. Lewis said much the same in arguing for our experience of God as being the source of our dogmatizing the trinitarian nature of God. He wrote (and I'll quote at some length):

> You may ask, 'If we cannot imagine a three-personal being, what is the good of talking about Him?' Well there isn't any good in talking about him. The thing that matters is being actually drawn into the 3-personal life, and that may begin any time—tonight if you like.

Lewis goes on to offer this experiential analogy:

> What I mean is this: An ordinary simple Christian kneels down to say his prayers. He is trying to get into touch with God. But if he is a Christian he knows that what is prompting him to pray is also God: God, so to speak, inside of him. But he also knows that all his real knowledge of God comes through Christ, the Man who was God—that Christ is standing beside him, helping him to pray, praying for him. You see what is happening. God is the thing to which he's praying—the goal he is trying to reach. God is also the thing inside of him which is pushing him on—the motive power. God is also the road or bridge along which he is being pushed to that goal. So that the whole three-fold way of life of the three-personal Being is actually going on in that ordinary little bedroom where an ordinary man is saying his prayers.[2]

And that's how theology started, Lewis concludes. People already knew God in a vague way. Then came a man who claimed to be God and he wasn't the kind of person you could dismiss as a lunatic. He made them believe him. They met him again after they'd seen him killed. And then, after they'd been formed into a little society or community, they found God inside them as well; directing them, making them able to do things they couldn't do before. And when they worked it all out they found they'd arrived at the Christian definition of the three-personal God.

The doctrine of the trinity, then, is a matter of experimental, experiential knowledge. Prior to dogma, an awful-sounding word that simply

---

2. Lewis, *Beyond Personality*, 10–11.

means doctrine or teaching, is the experience, an experience, Lewis maintains, that "spreads from person to person like a 'good infection.'"[3]

We, the church, are called to be a "contagious community," a gathering of folks through time and space infected with the life-giving Spirit of God, called to "pass it on." It was also Lewis, as I remember it, who once remarked that the problem with the "Christendom" mentality of the church of his day that still lingers on into our own, is that so many people have been inoculated with the weakest possible virus of Christian faith that they've developed an immunity of sorts and will never be in danger of coming down with a case of the real thing. And so our job as church, by the empowering Spirit, is to be viral agents spreading the trinitarian pandemic of salvation. It's an inelegant metaphor, I know, but so is H2O. To the old standbys, like "Holy, Holy, Holy" (*ELW #413*) which at least is based on today's text from Isaiah, try something both fresh and medieval as in the setting of Julian of Norwich's "Mothering God, You Gave Me Birth" (*ELW #735*).

Lectionary 8, Proper 3
(See Epiphany 8, Year B)

Lectionary 9, Proper 4

Psalm 81:1–10
Deuteronomy 5:12–15
2 Corinthians 4:5–12
Mark 2:23—3:6

I am the Lord God, who brought you up out of the land of Egypt.
Open your mouth wide and I will fill it.

—Psalm 81:10

---

3. Ibid., 11, 24.

Year B

The Sabbath

Today's Hebrew scripture reading from Deuteronomy and our Gospel reading from Mark collude in putting before us a curiously central but often ignored topic for preaching: the sabbath. Especially odd, perhaps, is to be commanded to rest—to "stop" as the Hebrew word for Sabbath literally orders—making a matter of law something we ought simply to delight in and find a wonderfully good piece of news, which it certainly is. "*Six days you shall labor and do all your work,*" the third commandment, by Lutheran and Roman Catholic reckoning, says. "*But the seventh day is a Sabbath to the Lord your God; you shall not do any work.*" But please notice that the commandment to observe the sabbath includes not just one's immediate family but "*your male or female slave, or your ox or your donkey, or any of your livestock, or the resident alien in your towns . . .*" What is God's rationale? It is to "*remember that you were a slave in the land of Egypt, and the Lord your God brought you out from there with a mighty hand and an outstretched arm . . .*" (vv 12–15).

In a sense, the sabbath is a weekly reminder of what passover celebrates annually, the Exodus, God's deliverance from Egypt. But with this difference: Israel is to recall the dangerous memory of its time of being slaves in Egypt, and so, the commandment implies, it is all important to provide the gift of sabbath to one's own slaves, to resident aliens and even one's livestock. I think it likely that the American Roman Catholic Bishops were inspired by this passage in their highly regarded Pastoral Letter on the Economy issued in the mid-eighties when they reminded their Catholic lay audience, now a largely affluent and comfortable part of mainstream American life, of how once American Catholics themselves were a poor immigrant minority often discriminated against by the Protestant majority. Don't forget from whence you've come when you consider matters of economic justice, they urged. Remember your origins; don't forget your "dangerous memories." Remember that it is God who made you who you are and that life is not an economic rat race.

But there is, you may remember, a second quite different, scriptural rationale for sabbath-keeping as well, rooted in the first creation account which closes on this note: "*And on the seventh day God finished the work that he had done, and he rested on the seventh day from all the work that he had done. So God blessed the seventh day and hallowed it, because on it God rested from all the work that he had done in creation*" (Gen 2:2–3). Do you get that? The text doesn't say, as we might assume, that God finished the creation in six days and rested on the seventh. Instead it says clearly that on the seventh day God *"finished"* the work of creation and rested. That is, as Rabbi Abraham Heschel has pointed out in his little masterwork *The Sabbath*, "the sabbath is itself the finishing," "the perfecting," "the completing of God's act of creation."[4] To take a day off and to rest from one's labors is the final act of creation, the ultimate creative deed in which we're invited—no, commanded—to participate. As YHWH in the thirty-first chapter of Exodus puts it, the sabbath *"is a sign for ever between me and the people of Israel that in six days the Lord made heaven and earth, and on the seventh day he rested, and was refreshed"* (v 17). Built into the very rhythm of nature, the text implies, as the culminating act of creation is sabbath rest—God's gift of refreshment.

We dare not make of the sabbath a utilitarian means to the end of making us better and harder workers, however, Heschel warns. "Man (sic) is not a beast of burden and the Sabbath is not for the purpose of enhancing the efficiency of his work." "The Sabbath is not an interlude but the climax of living." Six days a week we wrestle with the world, wringing profit from the earth; on the sabbath we especially care for the seed of eternity planted in the soul (the "image of God"). By this Heschel means, "there is a realm of time where the goal is not to have but to be, not to win but to give, not to control, but to share, not to subdue but to be in accord." The sabbath is "an armistice in man's cruel struggle for existence, a truce in all conflicts, personal and social." God created the sabbath, Heschel concludes in a memorable image, as a "sanctuary in time," "our great cathedral(s)" in the "architecture of time."[5]

It is clear from our Gospel text that the people of Israel found it no easier to keep the third commandment than the other nine, and that what it meant to remember the sabbath day to keep it holy could itself be a cause of great conflict among God's people. Here Jesus is taken to task by the Pharisees, the rigorists among the religious parties of Israel, for permitting on the sabbath his disciples to pluck grain and for himself healing a man with a withered hand both of which they took to be violations of the sabbath. Jesus himself first quotes scripture in support of his action and then asks the larger question, *"Is it lawful to do good or to do harm on the sabbath, to save life or to kill?"* (vv 2:25, 3:3).

4. Heschel, *Sabbath*, 10, 22.
5. Ibid., 14, 29, 8.

But Jesus' most telling word to the Pharisees serves well as a defense of all nit-picking efforts to "protect" the sabbath by going to the heart of its meaning: *"The sabbath was made for humankind, and not humankind for the sabbath,"* Jesus says, and then adds what we can't help but hear as a word of challenge, *"so the Son of Man is lord even of the sabbath"* (vv 27–28). The charge of being a sabbath-breaker would end up being one of the nails in Jesus' coffin, so to speak, but here Heschel serves to remind us that the Pharisees depicted in the Gospels were not necessarily representative of all Jewish believers. For, in fact, rabbis themselves warned against the "deification of the law" by its strictest observers and warned that "excessive piety may endanger the fulfillment of the essence of the law." One ancient rabbi even argued in words more than reminiscent of Jesus' own stricture, "The Sabbath is given unto you, not you unto the Sabbath" and "There is nothing more important, according to the Torah, than to preserve human life."[6] There aren't many good sabbath hymns beyond the oldie "O Day of Rest and Gladness" (*ELW* #521) but "Morning Has Broken" (*ELW* #556) comes close with its third verse including references to "Mine is the morning, born of the one light Eden saw play" and to "God's recreation of the new day."

Lectionary 10, Proper 5

Psalm 130
Genesis 3:8–15
2 Corinthians 4:13—5:1
Mark 3:20–35

If you, O Lord, should mark iniquities, Lord, who could stand?

—Psalm 130:3

---

6. Ibid., 17. For further Christian reflection on the sabbath see Postema *Catch Your Breath* and Edwards, *Sabbath Time*.

Postils for Preaching

The Religious Quest(ion)

The first interrogative we encounter in the Bible is not, as we humans might assume, "Where is God," what we "earthlings" assume to be *the* religious question. But the Bible's initial query is God's to make of the human ones created out of the *adamah* in God's image, and now hiding out in the Garden: "*Where are you?*" (v 9). Religion, it turns out, rightly conceived, is God's quest for us, not ours for God.

It's a wonderfully told tale, this story of our originating disobedience to God's Word. It's not so much a "fall" into sin that is being described as a leap into humankind's innate craving to become the creator of its own destiny, to disavow creature-hood, by knowing good and evil like God—and thereby making God's Word superfluous. As Dietrich Bonhoeffer once put it, the pious promise, "*you will become like God,*" a seemingly good thing, is essentially the serpent's "religious trick" that aims to cut out God, the "middleman," and God's mediating Word as the means of our enlightenment as to how to live morally.[7] It's not so much that we are inherently evil as there is something basically screwy about us mortals. There is that about us that we inherently sense is not quite right with our ability to both know and do the good. Something about us "misses the mark" as the Greek word for sin, "*hamartia,*" signifies.

For an alternative reading that savors the humor and anthropomorphic take on the Creator in the telling of the story, see the Yale literary critic, Harold Bloom's *The Book of J*. He has fun theorizing that the author of the Yahwist narrative must have been a woman, perhaps in Solomon's court, so light, playful and contrarian is her version of the creation story and its aftermath. Bloom considers the text not at all a "moral tale" but a "children's story that ends unhappily." "When we were children," he summarizes the essence of the story, "we were terribly punished for being children."[8]

A canny insight of Walter Brueggemann just might curb our own religious ambitions as we anticipate preaching on such a rich and well-known story. Think of the serpent, he suggests, as the creation's first theologian who convinces humankind to trade obedience to God's word for theology about God. As such it is a story that insinuates the warning that "theological talk which seeks to analyze and objectify matters of faithfulness is dangerous enterprise." Today's story from the book of beginnings further

---

7. Bonhoeffer, *Creation and Fall*, 67–69.
8. Bloom, *Book of J*, 185

shows how "anxiety comes from doubting God's providence, from rejecting his care and seeking to secure our own well-being." The serpent seduces humankind into believing there are securities apart from the reality of God, and so "failure to trust God with our lives" proves to be "death."[9]

If our Genesis story is about humankind's eternal hiding from God in its seemingly religious quest to become determiner of its own destiny by "finding" God, today's quizzical Gospel story has something of a "Where's Waldo?" quality to it in which Jesus' own family plays a leading role. "What's going on with our boy Jesus?" seems to be his family's concern as they fear he is being harassed by the crowds that are thronging before his very door, to the point that *they could not even eat.* Things were evidently getting out of control, and his family—including mother, who here makes her initial entrance into Mark's telling of the gospel—is about to make what we might call an "intervention" with Jesus. For the people were saying, *"He's gone out of his mind,"* whereas the learned scribes who had come down from Jerusalem—the certified smart people—had a diagnosis both more sophisticated and specific: *"He has Beelzebul, and by the ruler of the demons he casts out demons"* (vv 20–22).

Frankly, Jesus' responses, as Mark tells it, may not be any more convincing to contemporary hearers than to his original audience. Their conclusion could be ours: *"He has an unclean*—or at least "unclear"—*spirit."* His babbling about Satan casting out Satan and a kingdom divided against itself, about the need to tie up a strong man before plundering his house and then, finally, his words about blaspheming against the Holy Spirit as the only unforgivable sin (vv 23–30)—over which the church has been scratching its head ever since—all ought to give us more than pause.

But then the finale, with Jesus' mother and brothers (and some manuscripts add sisters) coming and asking for him at least ought to raise our eyebrows. And especially his chilly rebuff questioning who are my mother and brothers but those who do the will of God! There is no need homiletically to tie this all up in one neat bundle or even try to suggest why Mark is bothering to include this troubling and perplexing episode from Jesus' early ministry. Suffice it to suggest that there are unclear boundaries between mental illness and mental health, then and now, especially where things religious come into play. Could it be that even Jesus had his moments when his words and behavior could be variously interpreted, even by those who knew him and loved him best? And maybe—just maybe—the

---

9. Brueggemann, *Genesis*, 47–48, 54–55.

only prescription for our human malady first diagnosed in Genesis is to do the *"will of God"* by heeding God's Word while not succumbing to the allures of our native religiosity. So we *"do not lose heart"* is Paul's word for the day, admittedly taken out of context, even as it sometimes seems we may be losing our minds! Try the Tanzanian hymn "Listen, God is Calling" (*ELW* #513) or "Open Your Ears, O Faithful People (*ELW* #519) sung to a traditional Hasidic tune.

Lectionary 11, Proper 6

Psalm 92:1–4, 12–15
Ezekiel 17:22–24
2 Corinthians 5:6–10 [11–13] 14–17
Mark 4:26–34

*It is good to give thanks to the Lord,
to sing praises to your name, O Most High;
to declare your steadfast love in the morning,
and your faithfulness by night . . .*

—Psalm 92:1–2

Story-Telling Man

The chorus of a song entitled "The Parables" goes like this: "Story teller, yes he was the story-telling kind;/He painted pictures in their mind,/It was the way he let them see/How things were really meant to be."[10] It was only last week that we, for the first time in Mark's Gospel, were introduced to Jesus as a "story-telling man," one who not only healed, exorcized, and proclaimed the kingdom of God but did so *"in parables,"* as today's text puts it. In fact, it is one of the most characteristic things about Jesus so that Mark goes so far

---

10 Wilson, *He Lived the Good Life*, 63–65.

as to claim *"he did not speak to them except in parables,"* while adding *"but he explained everything in private to his disciples"* (v 34).

This would be a good Sunday to give your congregation a little taste of "parabolic" preaching which can go a long way toward loosening the grip of literalistic biblical interpretation that so afflicts many of our congregations. Start with a simple Greek word study that shows how *"parabole"* means to "throw something out alongside" of something else, and how metaphor and story-telling are essential to how the truth of the gospel grasps us. Of course I'm not recommending that you lecture your congregation on the niceties of religious language, but find a way to help folks to see how Jesus leads the way in his mode of preaching, teaching and acting so as to guide us into encounters with the non-literal, indirection of the gospel of the kingdom of God—itself, of course, a metaphor.[11]

My suspicion is that at least a part of the accusation we encountered last week of Jesus being out of his right mind may well have taken rise from his habitual parable-telling mode of teaching which avoided answering direct questions and instead resorted to the inventive telling of odd tales, many without an obvious point or moral, which nonetheless limned the eccentric reality of what God's kingdom is like. Today we find Jesus using one of his favorite images that will recur in many of his stories, that of the seed and then, more particularly, the mustard seed, common enough agricultural allusions even to Jerusalem religious grandees in attendance. The mustard seed, among the smallest of seeds, becomes the greatest of shrubs when grown, sufficiently large that *"the birds of the air can make nests in their shade"* (v 32). One of my most vivid memories as a young boy is pulling mustard plants (yellow weeds) out of the oats field of my friend Bobby's father's farm, and, indeed, upsetting the raucous birds who had nested in them. This is what parables do: they activate our imagination and memory and invite us to make connections with God's "really real," rooting the kingdom of God in our earthly realities.

Our Hebrew scripture text from Ezekiel may well have been in Jesus' mind as he threw out the image of the mustard seed to his audience. For here the prophet is speaking of God's action as a transplanting of a sprig which becomes, in time, a noble cedar tree under which *"every kind of bird will live . . . and nest"* (v 23). This image immediately sets my mind reeling off to the beautiful Navajo woven tree-of-life rugs I've seen, to the intricate and delicate Egyptian parchment-like tree, branches filled with all kinds of

---

11. See, for example, Gunton's *Actuality of the Atonement*.

birds, a much-valued piece of artwork given me as a gift on the occasion of their baptisms by Arash, Tani and Bamdad originally from Teheran. Or think too of other scriptural trees from Eden to John's Revelation. This is the way our minds work, free associating God's kingdom from a suggestive image. This is dangerous territory, of course, for who can control where an image will take us—or the kingdom of God, for that matter? Here the hymn by Eric Routley, "There in God's Garden" (*ELW* #342) occurs to me as a fitting choice with its recurring tree imagery.

God's kingdom that Jesus evokes in our minds is an alternative reality that is subversive, elusive, and undermining to our normal ways of being. I can't help but think of Woody Allen's movie, "The Purple Rose of Cairo" where the Jeff Daniels character strides right out of the movie, off the cinema screen, into the audience to sit next to the Mia Farrow character who has become so entranced with the film and fallen in love with Daniels' character. The rest of the film is a story of the confrontation and conflict between these two realities. Farrow's character sums it all up as she enthuses to a friend about her encounter: "I've just met the most marvelous man. Of course he's fictional. But you can't have everything!"

We Christians, of course, believe that the kingdom of God is the "really real," the already-in-our-midst, though hidden, reality pulling us into God's good future that Jesus evoked, embodied, and promised to bring to fruition. The church is God's "mustard seed conspiracy," as someone once described it. I remember seeing many years ago a banner in a prison chapel that posed the troubling question in nicely confrontational, metaphorical language: "If you were charged with being a Christian would there be enough evidence to convict you?" As we find Paul putting it to the Corinthian church in today's reading, *"we walk by faith, not by sight . . . So if anyone is in Christ, there is a new creation: everything old has passed away; see everything has become new!"* (vv 7, 17). "We Walk By Faith" (*ELW* #635) sets Paul's words to a singable Marty Haugen tune.

Year B

Lectionary 12, Proper 7

Psalm 107:1–3, 23–32
Job 38:1–11
2 Corinthians 6:1–13
Mark 4:35–41

Some went down to the sea in ships,
doing business on the mighty waters;
they saw the deeds of the Lord,
his wondrous works in the deep.
For he commanded and raised the stormy wind,
which lifted up the waves of the sea.

—PSALM 107:23–25

Fear and Faith

Let's admit it. We want it both ways. We want both a just God who is all-powerful and not only is the creator but the controller of nature, as well as a benevolent God who doesn't pull the strings of nature or keep account of natural and human events according to some simple moral calculus of rewarding the good and punishing the evil. My preference is to opt for the mysterious "both . . . and" perspective offered in the ultimate chapter of Genesis in which Joseph is found articulating to his conniving, mistrustful brothers a theological perspective on evil that refuses to name God its author but does credit the maker of all with sufficient creativity so as to be able to use evil as the raw material for good (see Gen 50:19–21).

Joseph's is a theological perspective much needed in our day of natural disasters and threatened ecological catastrophe, not to speak of ongoing acts of terrorism, war, violent crime and the displacement of millions of people become refugees from all of these causes. God is not to blame, but God is in the business of using natural catastrophes and human evil as the clay for molding a new creation. Today's reading from the book of Job offers a singular opportunity to reflect on the age-old issue of theodicy or how to account for the presence of evil in a world created by a loving and just God. Like the Jesus of the Gospels, God is not to be seen as the "answer man" but as the one who puts to us the question, *"Where were you when I laid the foundations of the earth?"* (v 4). In other words, our questions of God, including questions regarding God's fairness and justice and goodness, need to be put in perspective—in God's perspective. To coin a neo-logism, what's really needed is a thoroughgoing "anthropo-dicy," that probes from a Word-informed perspective our human predilection for wanting to know good and evil like God without the ability to do the good we do know, as Paul once put it to the Romans (7:15–21).

Shortly after returning to live and work in California, a little more than a decade ago, I finally got around to reading a classic of American literature, Richard Henry Dana's *Two Years Before the Mast*. In this engaging, first-person account of a young Harvard undergraduate's two-year voyage on a merchant schooner around Cape Horn from Boston to California and back in the mid-1830's, the reader is simply swamped with the multifarious perils that endangered seafarers of an earlier age—from mountainous icebergs to raging typhoons, from the attacks of gargantuan whales to marauding pirates, from the physical ailments of scurvy and serious shipboard injuries to the cruel lashings of a despotic captain. This, indeed, was the dangerous and adventurous life of those who, as the Psalmist put it over two and a half millennia ago, *"went down to the sea in ships, doing business on the mighty waters"* (v 23). Compare, too, Paul's catalogue of afflictions cited in today's second reading that he faced as a "servant of God" (vv 4–5). Whether you live in sight of water or not, it's certainly a day to sing together what's traditionally known as the "Navy Hymn," "Eternal Father, Strong to Save" (*ELW* #756) with its refrain, "Oh, hear us when we cry to thee/For those in peril on the sea."

The Sea of Galilee, by all accounts, is much more a lake than an ocean, but a sudden storm can still be a frightening experience, even for a group of disciples, several of whom had been known to make their living as fishermen on these same waters. In this telling of the story, the disciples interrupt Jesus' well-earned nap by awakening him during the storm that threatens to swamp their boat with an accusing question: *"Teacher, do you not care that we are perishing?"* It's another of those complex questions we learned about in logic class to which there is no good answer, as in "When did you stop kicking your dog?"

But however rudely awakened, Jesus ignores the disciples and directly "*rebuked the wind and said to the sea,*" Mark reports, "*Peace! Be still!*" I think a better translation would be "Calm down!" and "Be quiet!", words that I expect while directed to the inanimate wind and sea were meant to be overheard by his frantic disciples who so rudely had disturbed his sleep. At any rate, "*the wind ceased and there was a dead calm,*" but I expect the disciples quieted down as well. For it's to them that Jesus now turns and asks the questions, "*Why are you afraid? Have you still no faith?*"(vv 38–40). Both are questions, notice, asked in the present tense. Not "Why *were* you afraid?" or "*Had* you no faith?" but "Why *are* you fearful and faithless?" It's a present-tense question that includes you and me.

Mark ends the episode on an even more curious note as he observes: "*And they were filled with great awe and said to one another, 'Who then is this that even the wind and the sea obey him?'*"(v 41). Again a weak English translation, "*filled with great awe,*" leads us to ignore the ironic intensity of the Greek word for fear, "*phobos,*" by literally saying "they feared a great fear," "awe," perhaps, being an aspect of such fear but losing the sense of fright connected to the furious wind and waves that had been endangering them. The episode rightly leaves the disciples' unanswered question hanging, a tantalizing hint to the answer of Mark's "messianic secret," "Who then is this, that even the wind and the sea obey him?" Who indeed? Stay tuned for next week's installment. "Jesus, Savior, Pilot Me" (*ELW* #755) is another oldie but goodie, sea-song for land-lubbing Christians, as is the simple, contemporary verse refrain, "Calm to the Waves," (*ELW* #794).

Lectionary 13, Proper 8

Psalm 30
Lamentations 3:22–33
2 Corinthians 8:7–15
Mark 5:21–43

To you, O Lord, I cried, and to the Lord I made supplication:
'What profit is there in my death, if I go down to the Pit?
Will the dust praise you? Will it tell of your faithfulness?'

—Psalm 30:8–9

Lament

"Lament" is a word we don't use much in everyday conversation, or, for that matter, hear very much in church. In fact, the Hebrew scripture reading for this morning is one of the rare times in our three-year lectionary that we hear from the little-known, five-chapter long book of the Bible. "Lamentations," as the book is called in English, simply takes its Hebrew title from its first word—really just a sigh, "Ah, how . . . " In its Greek translation it's simply entitled "Wailings."

We've all seen on television news scenes of Middle Eastern funerals and of the public wailing that accompanies the rituals surrounding death in semitic cultures. In ancient times the dirge or lament was a common poetic form, and the book of Lamentations is an especially advanced form of such art, particularly insofar as much of it, including today's reading, is an acrostic or alphabetic poem where each verse begins with a successive letter of the Hebrew alphabet, moving from aleph through taw.[12]

Historically, the book of Lamentations was written, it's timely to note on this Sunday before our Fourth of July—the national "holy day" of American civil religion—as a lament bewailing the fall of Jerusalem and the destruction of the temple in 587 BCE and the ensuing exile of many of the people of Judah who were carted off to Babylon—modern-day Iraq. It's a national catastrophe that's being mourned, you see, but one certainly also experienced on a deeply personal level as a tragedy, in the Greek sense, in which the people of Judah are in a strong sense to blame, as prophets like Jeremiah and Hosea, Isaiah and Ezekiel had warned.

Most of the first chapters of Lamentations are full of unrelieved doom and gloom—some of it blaming God, some of it confessing guilt, some of it pleading for help—a medley of emotions not all that unlike the so-called "stages of death and dying" that Elizabeth Kubler-Ross claimed to have identified—denial, anger, bargaining, depression and finally acceptance,[13] acceptance marked by hope being the longed-for final stage. It's the stage that the biblical lamenter seems at last to have reached in our appointed text for today. But—and it's a big "but"—this good news that God's mercies are *"new every morning"* is only good for us once we've faced the bad news of our condition, once we've confronted honestly the negativity of life lived

---

12. See Harrison, *Jeremiah and Lamentations* 195–203 as well as Davidson, *Jeremiah and Lamentations*, Vol II 167–172.

13. Kubler-Ross, *On Death and Dying*.

in the face of death and our death-dealing ways, once we've acknowledged our need to grieve and lament.

Walter Brueggemann puts its this way: "It is clear that a church that goes on singing 'happy songs' in the face of raw reality is doing something very different from what the Bible itself does . . ." For in doing so, he goes on, it is ". . . less an evangelical defiance guided by faith, and much more a frightened, numb denial and deception that does not want to acknowledge or experience the disorientation of life." Quite to the contrary, Brueggemann affirms that to lament, in the strong biblical sense, "is an act of bold faith because it insists that the world must be experienced as it really is and not in some pretended way." "On the other hand," he continues, "it is bold because it insists that all such experiences of disorder are proper subject for discourse with God. There is nothing out of bounds, nothing precluded or inappropriate."[14]

Consider, for example, today's appointed Psalm 30 in which the Psalmist bares his distressed soul to God in prayer, in effect, bargaining with God: *"To you, O Lord, I cried, and to the Lord I made supplication: 'What profit is there in my death, if I go down to the Pit? Will the dust praise you? Will it tell of your faithfulness?'"* (vv 8–9). Or think of the opening verse of Psalm 130 *"Out of the depths I cry to you, O Lord"* (v 1) or, most famously, Jesus' cry of dereliction from the cross borrowed from the opening strophe of Psalm 22 *"My God, my God, why have you forsaken me?"* (v 1). This is exactly the crux of brother Martin's distinction between a theology of the cross, which he once said "calls a thing what it really is," as over against a theology of glory, a "theology of the happy face," I call it, which Luther said calls evil good and good evil.[15] And so, especially amid our officially optimistic American culture and its favored brand of upbeat religiosity, we need to realize that the affirmation of the gospel to which the lamenter finally works his way is a hard-won word of grace, a good word that is good precisely because it has weathered the storm, has entered into the darkness, has encountered death and the death-dealing forces of our world: *"The steadfast love of the Lord never ceases, his mercies never come to an end; they are new every morning"* (vv 22–23a).

---

14. Brueggemann, *Message of the Psalms*, 51–52.

15. See again Forde, *On Being a Theologian of the Cross* and its epigraph taken from Luther's *Heidelberg Disputation*: "The thirst for glory is not ended by satisfying it but rather by extinguishing it."

Let me tell you one of my favorite lament stories. My mother once asked me to pay a visit to an old family friend who was hospitalized with very serious kidney disease. Jesse was the mother of my old boyhood friend, Gary, so of course I said I'd be happy to do so. Entering her hospital room I was shocked to see this one-time tall and imposing farm woman—a shirt-tail cousin of my father—lying pale and emaciated in her hospital bed. Still, she smiled at me in recognition as I pulled over a chair, took her hand and asked her, as I usually do, "How're you doing, Jessie?" And to my considerable surprise out poured a sharp and poignant stream of complaint and grief and lament such as I'd rarely encountered, particularly at such length and from someone so evidently on the precipice of death.

I don't remember precisely, but I think I probably then read Psalm 71, when she had spent herself and calmed down a bit, a song of lament itself in the voice of an older person that pleads in part, *"So even to old age and gray hairs, O God, do not forsake me . . ."* And then I shared prayer and holy communion and God's blessing with Jessie.

As I got up to say goodbye and a word of benediction, fully aware that this would probably be my last visit with her, Jessie looked at me with a wan smile and uttered her own good words, "Thanks, John, for coming—it means a lot." And then she added with a hint of apology in her voice, "You know, my pastors are good about visiting me, but after driving thirty-five miles one-way into the city, they think it's their job to cheer me up. But you just listened to me. Thanks for that."

And thanks to Jessie and her words of benediction, for I'll be forever grateful for her honesty in letting me know how important it is for us to truly lament, as a pastor to simply shut up and invite the other to share what's going on as a ground rule in pastoral care. I remember a pastoral colleague who told the story of how before praying, she always asked the person being visited whether she/he had something special they'd like for her to pray. Once a woman, without blinking an eye, said something to the effect, "You know what I really need more than anything is a bowel movement." That's not exactly lament but it's certainly real and honest. And true to the Jesus we find rushing around in today's reading, responding to myriad needs with grace and compassion—and even a bit of humor (See my postil "Ministry by Interruption," Lectionary 10, Year A). Hymns of lament aren't legion, but try the newish "How Long, O God" (*ELW* #698), "When Pain of the World Surrounds Us" (*ELW* #704), and "In Deepest Night" (*ELW* #699).

Year B

Lectionary 14, Proper 9

Psalm 123
Ezekiel 2:1–5
2 Corinthians 12:2–10
Mark 6:1–13

*Have mercy upon us, O Lord, have mercy upon us
for we have had more than enough of contempt.
Our soul has had more than its fill of the scorn of those who are at ease,
of the contempt of the proud.*

—PSALM 123:3–4

Prophets or Profits?

July is the month of prophets as we hear today in our Hebrew scripture reading from Ezekiel, next week from Amos, and then from Jeremiah and Elisha in succeeding weeks. It is a good, extended opportunity to reflect on the role of the prophet in ancient Israel, and I recommend taking some time to renew your familiarity with the prophetic tradition using time-tested resources like Abraham Heschel's *The Prophets* or Martin Buber's *The Prophetic Faith* as well as the work of more contemporary scholars. For Christian preachers, of course, this provides the occasion to see both Jesus and John the Baptizer within the tradition of Israel's prophets of old and to consider how God continues to send us prophets in our own day.

Our reading from Ezekiel is a good place to start since we hear the story of the prophet's own initial call from God while limning some of the difficulties of the prophetic vocation which others will also encounter. Ezekiel begins by describing how "*a spirit entered into me and set me on my feet.*" The prophetic summons is one that comes from outside of oneself—it is not self-initiated—and, in fact, is often resisted by the recipient (see Jeremiah!). It comes as a calling, Ezekiel goes on to describe, that is a "*sending*" to the people of Israel with a "*Thus says the Lord God*" (vv 3–4). These are words the Word-bearing prophet cannot expect will be welcomed but will likely be both resisted and rejected by God's *"rebellious," "impudent,"* and *"stubborn"* people. And yet, *"whether they hear or refuse to hear,"* the prophet is assured, *"they shall know that there has been a prophet among them"* (v 5). In other words, the success of the prophet's mission is not to be measured by whether the word of the Lord is heeded but whether it is spoken faithfully. This is a word the church of every age needs to hear. As a prophet of the exile would declare on God's behalf memorably: *"so shall my word be that goes forth from my mouth; it shall not return to me empty, but it shall accomplish that which I purpose, and succeed in the thing for which I sent it"* (Isa 55:11).

Today's Gospel reading from Mark 6 tells the story of Jesus' return to his hometown, better known from Luke 4 as Jesus' inaugural sermon. Here too he astounds the crowd of homies with his teaching. These home town folks can't help but wonder where this local *"carpenter, the son of Mary"* with all his brothers and sisters present right here with them, got this wisdom and power. *"And they took offense at him"* (vv 1–3). Mark says, meaning literally in Greek, they found him a *"scandalon"* or stumbling block.

What really scandalized his hometown folks was Jesus' flippant throwing in their faces the old proverb, *"Prophets are not without honor, except in their hometown, and among their own kin, and in their own house"* (v 4). Here we find Jesus both, in effect, assuming the prophetic mantle and flaunting it in the face of his old friends and family who assumed they knew him so well. And so, *"amazed at their unbelief,"* Jesus shook off the dust of his feet against them where he *"could do no deed of power"* (vv 5–6) anyway—except the curing of a few people—and bid his disciples to go out and do likewise, which they did with some success.

I often wonder how the early church and its Gospel writers found the courage to describe Jesus the great teacher and prophet so honestly as one who failed to convince so many of the truth of his teaching—including, often enough, his own disciples. At the very least those of us who have had our difficult moments in confirmation instruction or stabs at prophetic preaching here might find some consolation. Faithfulness to the prophetic word rather than success in creating a positive response to it is clearly God's criterion.

This week normally containing the Fourth of July holiday provides the context in which to be reminded that true prophets always speak God's word into the midst of the messy politics of their day. Try reminding folks, for example, of the famous words of Abraham Lincoln's "Second Inaugural Address" spoken just weeks before his assassination on Good Friday, 1865. Here he invoked God's mysterious will as a prophetic word that alone could provide perspective for the way ahead for an America that was still at war with itself.[16] Reading the same Bible and praying to the same God as both sides did, Lincoln admitted, only complicated the matter. Yet, he promised, "The Almighty has his purposes" and "the judgments of the Lord are true and righteous altogether."

Do you feel called to utter a prophetic word from God directed into the midst of the messiness of our contemporary world? If so, gird yourself and pluck up your courage, as William Sloane Coffin, Jr. once warned us more timid word-bearers in his prophetic-sounding adage, "Hell is truth seen too late."[17] Take courage from the assurance Paul testified to having received from God through his own *"thorn in the flesh"* that *"my grace is sufficient for you, for my power is made perfect in weakness"* (v 9). And then wait for the fireworks. "God Has Spoken by His Prophets" (*LBW* #238) is one of few hymns that sings of the prophets.

Lectionary 15, Proper 10

Psalm 85:8–13
Amos 7:7–15
Ephesians 1:3–14
Mark 6:14–29

Steadfast love and faithfulness will meet;
righteousness and peace will kiss each other.

—PSALM 85:10

---

16. See, for example, White's *Lincoln's Greatest Speech*.
17. *Credo*, 53.

God's Plumb Line

A vision given Amos, an eighth-century prophet, was that of God standing beside a wall, plumb-line in hand. This provided a vivid picture of God's own sense of righteousness (also known as "justice" or simple "straightness/rightness") by which Israel's actions were to be measured and rectified. The history of God's chosen people was one rife with acts of "crookedness," that is, behaviors, decisions, and actions that had "fallen out of plumb" with God's expectations. Prophets of the ilk of Amos, (an alien farm worker with no prophetic pedigree), found wielding God's plumb-line an onerous, unrewarding task. It meant incurring the accusation of the northern kingdom of Israel's religious establishment that he was at the heart of a conspiracy against the very king of Israel. Amaziah, a priest of the king's sanctuary in Bethel, spoke more truthfully than he knew, like countless spokespeople for establishment religion after him (including a certain high priest named Caiphas), when he proclaimed of Amos, "*the land is not able to bear all his words*" (v 10).

Today's Gospel reading tells the story in flashback style of an Amos-come-lately of more than eight hundred years later who also dared to wield God's plumb-line against those in power and was made to suffer for it. Some, it seems, were beginning to think of Jesus of Nazareth as a kind of John the Baptizer *redivivus*, for the same "*powers*" were detected as being "*at work in him*" as if he were a latter-day Elijah or another of the "*prophets of old*" (vv 14–15). For conventional religionists of the day, prophets were believed to be a phenomenon of the past—and the farther in the past the better! King Herod led the way in jumping to the conclusion on hearing reports of Jesus that it could only mean, "*John, whom I beheaded, has been raised*" (v 16).

Mark uses Herod's remark as a segue to narrate the details of a story both so sexy and gory that it has provided titillation not only to generations of Sunday school children but even has inspired the likes of Oscar Wilde and Richard Strauss. Herod (also called "Antipas") here is not quite the villain we expect in light of his "Great" father's notorious cruelty exhibited in the slaughter of the Bethlehem innocents as well as numerous others, as the historian Josephus catalogues his atrocities. Rather, it is his former sister-in-law (whom he had married illicitly) who carried a grudge against John's wielding of God's plumb-line against her marital shenanigans. And so she successfully connives to have her daughter so enthrall Antipas with her wiles as a dancer that an otherwise reluctant king promises to grant her anything she might request. John's head on a platter turns out to be her mother's first choice. And so, through this lurid tale, we learn the story of John's grisly death which Mark concludes in an artful manner, eerily prefiguring the story of yet another politically motivated death soon to follow in his Gospel narrative: "*they came and took his body, and laid it in a tomb*" (v 29).

The real prophetic conspiracy of which Amos, John, and Jesus, were a part ("conspiracy" literally meaning a "breathing together") is of God's inspiration ("breathing into"). The writer of Ephesians goes so far as to call it a "*mystery,*" God's "*plan for the fullness of time*" (vv 9–10) which subverts any and all establishment religion that assumes there can be such a thing as a "*king's sanctuary*" or a "*temple of the kingdom*" (Amos 7:9). Instead, the "*mystery*" and "*plan*" God "*has made known to us*" is "*set forth in Christ*" as God's intention to "*gather up all things in him, things in heaven and on earth*" (v 10). The Greek word "*anakephalaiosastai*" is not only a mouthful to pronounce but, as Dan Erlander has enthused in his book *Manna and Mercy*,[18] it is an immensely rich word that means not only "to gather up" as translated in the NRSV but also God's uniting and bringing together the whole creation. God's "mending of the cosmos" was Krister Stendahl's favorite way of putting it—God's "*tikkun,*" in Hebrew. "*In him we have redemption through his blood, the forgiveness of our trespasses, according to the riches of his grace that he lavished on us*" (v 7) is Ephesians' way of describing this "*oikonomian*" of God—God's "economy of salvation."

Few have put it better than the Danish writer Karen Blixen, known best by her pen name of Isak Dinesen. In the climactic scene of her short story "Babette's Feast," (also made into an award-winning film of the same name), she put these words into the mouth of one of her characters who is making a kind of banquet speech which takes today's psalmody as its text (they're words I've quoted above, as well, in another context):

> Mankind, my friends, is frail and foolish. We have all of us been told that grace is to be found in the universe. But in our human foolishness and shortsightedness we imagine divine grace to be finite... But the moment comes when our eyes are opened, and we see and realize that grace is infinite. Grace, my friends, demands nothing from us but that we shall await it with confidence and acknowledge it in gratitude... Grace takes us all to its bosom and proclaims general amnesty. See! That which we have chosen is

---

18. 77, 93

given us, and that which we have refused is, also and at the same time, granted us. Ay that which we have rejected is poured upon us abundantly. For mercy and truth have met together and righteousness and bliss have kissed one another.¹⁹

"Thy Strong Word" (*ELW* #511) is a compelling hymn extolling God's incendiary Word set to a stark melody unusual for its repeated triplets. But sing too the popular Tanzanian hymn "Listen, God is Calling" (*ELW* #513).

Lectionary 16, Proper 11

Psalm 23
Jeremiah 23:1–6
Ephesians 2:11–22
Mark 6:30–34, 53–56

The Lord is my shepherd, I shall not want . . .
He leads me in right paths for his name's sake.

—Psalm 23:1, 3

A Sunday in Nanjing

In July of 1997 I found myself in the most unusual and challenging preaching situation of my entire ministry. The situation was this: Exhausted and exhilarated by eight solid days of meetings and Bible study and worship and small group discussions held in Hong Kong (with a bit of playing tourist on the side), just a week after the hand-over from British to Chinese sovereignty, our post-Lutheran World Federation delegation of eighteen had arrived in Nanjing, China for a five-day visit hosted by the China Christian Council. Upon our arrival, our hosts informed us that one of us would need to serve as preacher for the worship service we would be attending as a

---

19. Dinesen, "Babette's Feast," 60–61.

group on Sunday morning in one of Nanjing's largest churches. I—the lone American and unknown to anyone else in our multi-national group—was quickly identified and agreed upon as the designated preacher. Perhaps this was as an act of ecclesiastical anti-Americanism, but the stated rationale was that I, being the only native English-speaker of the group, all of the rest of whom understood English, it would be simplest for me to preach in English, with only Chinese translation needed for the rest of the congregation.

This logic seemed to make sense to the group, and while I was not wild about having to prepare a sermon from scratch on short notice in the midst of a busy schedule with my Bible as my only resource, I agreed. (The truth of the matter, I suspect, is that like any group of pastors, no one wanted the hard work of writing and preaching a sermon under such conditions.) My only directives were first, that I would need to pick my own sermon text and second, the sermon should not be too short—the only time before or since I have ever received that particular warning. As a lectionary preacher it was only natural to begin my search for a text by looking at the appointed readings for the coming Sunday in our American lectionary, and *voila!*, it was as though the Spirit had selected the perfect reading for this anxiety-provoking occasion. The sermon quickly seemed to write itself, so fitting the text proved: Ephesians 2:11–22, the second reading for today. On Sunday morning, just preceding the service I met with the local Chinese pastor who, perhaps sensing my anxiety, grinned at me and said "You know that this congregation is named 'Moo Shoo Road Church' which in English means "Don't Worry Road Church." Again, the Spirit provides!

I began my sermon by noting how the Ephesians, being "*Gentiles by birth*," are in the letter addressed as those who prior to Christ were considered "*aliens*" and "*strangers*" to Israel's "*covenants of promise*" (vv 11–12). This, I said, is something that both our international delegation as well as most American Christians have in common with Chinese Christians. "Germans and Poles, Indians, Indonesians and Malaysians, South Africans and Ethiopians and Americans—as well as the Chinese people—are all aliens and strangers to God's covenant promises of old. None of us non-Jews can claim priority in God's eyes." Dusting off a little church history, I went on: "But as our Ethiopian friends can testify, the Gospel took root in Ethiopia long before the German tribes ever heard of Jesus" (a gentle tweaking of my German Lutheran colleagues) "and the Gospel was proclaimed in India and China, a millennium before Columbus sailed for the so-called 'new world.'" This was our common starting point as Gentiles, non-Jewish Christians.

But the good news as radically articulated in Ephesians is that *"in Christ Jesus you who once were far off have been brought near by the blood of Christ. For he is our peace"* (vv 13–14). This is good news for all *"strangers"* and *"aliens."* Our Chinese hosts had taken our delegation to see the ancient Nanjing city wall and its famous China Gate, built to protect Nanjing from invaders—"a most impressive testimony in brick and mortar to the ingenuity of your forbears," I went on. "Yet this massive wall was unable to protect your city from the horrible and infamous Nanjing Massacre" whose memorial we had also visited. The Good News of Ephesians is that God *"has broken down the dividing wall, that is, the hostility between us . . . that he might create in himself one new humanity . . . thus making peace . . . through the cross, thus putting to death that hostility through it"* (vv 15–17).

"Our scripture puts it in even stronger language: we are to consider ourselves bricks—building blocks—of God's temple, the church, we call it, built upon the foundation of the apostles and prophets and all those saints who have gone before us. But, most importantly, with Jesus Christ as the cornerstone—the One on whom the whole building relies for its strength and stability and security" (vv 19–21). I concluded: "We pray that you—with us—as individual believers and as churches—may become building blocks for God's kingdom—God's perfect reign of peace and justice for which we wait and work here and now, confident that God the architect and builder, will find us suitable building material for God's spiritual temple—the sanctuary and hope for all creation. And that as you also in Christ Jesus are called to witness to your fellow Chinese, you might also be a witness to us in the rest of the world."

Never had I experienced a text interfacing quite so seamlessly with its present context, proclaiming the good news of Jesus Christ in fresh, vivid, and yet utterly authentic and simple biblical language. It was a text that certainly preached! Sermon ended, by now drenched in sweat as I climbed down from the pulpit, someone went to the rickety old piano at the front of the church and began plunking out a familiar melody in which all those assembled soon joined their voices as we sang together in Chinese and English "What a Friend We Have in Jesus" (*ELW* #742), the one we all felt in that moment of grace who indeed was the Good Shepherd showing care and compassion for all his flock whatever their origin (Psalm 23, Jeremiah 23, and Mark 8:34b).

Year B

Lectionary 17, Proper 12

Psalm 145:10–18
2 Kings 4:42–44
Ephesians 3:14–21
John 6:1–21

The eyes of all look to you, and you give them their food in due season. You open your hand, satisfying the desire of every living thing.

—PSALM 145:15–16

Companions

The story of the "Feeding of the Five Thousand" that begins our five-week long foray into the sixth chapter of John's Gospel is the only miracle of Jesus recorded in all four Gospels. I wonder why. What's so special about this of all stories about Jesus that made the cut and got into the Bible in four slightly different versions? The very last verse of John's Gospel reads: *"There are also many other things that Jesus did; if every one of them were written down, I suppose that the world itself could not contain the books that would be written"* (21:25). This need not be just a rhetorical question but can be a good opener to an audience-participation sermon.

In John's Gospel it's so special that it's used as a prelude to Jesus' long, rambling "bread of life" theme that we'll be considering until the end of August during these dog days of summer. In John's telling of the tale the story begins with Jesus, not the disciples, raising the question of Philip (in order to "test" him, the text says): *"Where are we to buy bread for these people to eat?"* This tips us off that what follows is meant as instruction for Philip and his fellow disciples. Philip's answer was a common sense enough reply, *"Six months wages wouldn't buy enough bread for each of them to get a little."* But Andrew, Simon Peter's brother, pipes up, perhaps having anticipated the problem and done a little reconnaissance of the crowd, *"There is a child here who has five barley loaves and two fish. But what are they among so many?"*

(vv 5–9). But in Jesus' hands, a little can mean a lot, seeming scarcity can become the occasion of prodigal plenty.

And so, John tells us, in words we can't help but hear echoes of the rhythms of the narrative of that last supper Jesus would share with his friends according to the synoptic and Pauline accounts of the tradition but not, interestingly, in John's story of that final meal, Jesus *"took the loaves, and when he had given thanks, he distributed to them who were seated. And so also the fish, as much as they wanted."* When they were satisfied he told his disciples to gather up whatever was left over, *"so that nothing may be lost."* And, wonder of wonders, the left-overs filled twelve baskets. The point is the powerful prodigality of Jesus' blessing in which "not enough" becomes "more than enough," where God's surprising plenty utterly overwhelms our sense of proportion and we all become "companions," "*companeros*" in Spanish, meaning literally "those who share bread together."[20]

Our other readings for today include the Hebrew scripture story of the prophet Elisha presiding over a miraculous meal multiplied by God out of minimal resources that clearly seems a template for our Gospel story. But it is the reading from Ephesians that supplies us with words of benediction that serve to expand our comprehension of the magnificent prodigality of God's grace. It's a Pauline antidote to the problem J.B Phillips years ago diagnosed in his little book *Your God is Too Small* which argued that modern folks are in the habit of underestimating God's power, of whittling God down to our own puny human size in order to fit our own human religious needs and desires and preconceptions rather than letting God be God. The author of Ephesians way of putting it in devotional language is, *"I pray that you may have the power to comprehend, with all the saints, what is the breadth and length and height and depth, and to know the love of Christ that surpasses knowledge, so that you may be filled with all the fullness of God"* (vv 18–19).

This expansive sense of God's prodigious graciousness, we also experienced several weeks back in the hard-won affirmation we heard from the Book of Lamentations: *"The steadfast love of the Lord never ceases, his mercies never end; they are new every morning . . . "* (3:22–23). Ephesians similarly "magnifies" God's prodigality in these words that you would do well to use as liturgical benediction upon a congregation that has become a community of *companeros* in its hearing of the feeding of the five thousand

---

20. See here Palmer's *Active Life*, 121–138 and my postil for Lectionary 18, Year A in which I retell a story I once heard Palmer tell based on this text.

and in its own feeding together on the bread of life promised in Jesus' meal: *"Now to him who by the power at work within us is able to accomplish abundantly far more than all we can ask or imagine, to him be glory in the church and in Christ Jesus to all generations, forever and ever. Amen"* (v 32). More than we can ask or imagine!

If you can find a hymn more fitting than the oldie "There's a Wideness in God's Mercy" (*ELW* #587) then sing it! But it's hard to out-do the line that begins verse 3, "For the love of God is broader than the measures of our mind" and then moves on to "But we make this love too narrow by false limits of our own;/ and we magnify its strictness with a zeal God will not own."

Lectionary 18, Proper 13

Psalm 78:23–29
Exodus 16:2–4, 9–15
Ephesians 4:1–16
John 6:24–35

Yet he commanded the skies above, and opened the doors of heaven;
He rained down on them manna to eat, and gave them the grain of heaven.
Mortals ate of the bread of angels; he sent them food in abundance.

—Psalm 78:23–25

What's It?

"What's it?" wondered the band of newly-liberated slaves, illegal aliens escaped from Egypt, now wanderers in the wilderness of Sinai. What is this stuff, this *"fine flaky substance, as fine as frost on the ground"* that God had sent them in response to their incessant grumbling over the rumbling in their stomachs that led to their mutinous complaint against Moses and Aaron, their YHWH-appointed leaders: *"If only we had died by the hand of* the Lord in the land of Egypt, when we sat by the fleshpots and ate our fill of bread; for you have brought us out into this wilderness to kill this whole assembly with hunger." And so YHWH sent quails in the evening and manna in the morning, which as Moses explained, "*is the bread that the Lord has given you to eat*" (vv 13–14, 3, 15). "Manna," as the "*flaky substance*" came to be called, funnily enough, simply takes its name from the Israelite's question, the word meaning literally "what's it?"

Truth to tell, as the Book of Numbers further explains, manna itself grew old fast to the tastes of these galloping gourmets (who knows what happened to the quail?) and we find the Israelites, in a passage we'll be hearing in a couple of months, complaining now of the unrelenting menu of manna. Here the yearning for the fleshpots of Egypt while beginning with the lament, "*If we only had meat to eat!*" expands to include: "*We remember the fish we used to eat in Egypt for nothing, the cucumbers, the melons, the leeks, the onions, and the garlic*"—oh, the garlic!—"*but now our strength is dried up, and there is nothing at all but this manna to look at*" (11:4–6). That's gratitude for you, which goes to show that even such "bread from heaven," as Jesus will call manna in today's Gospel reading, quickly can grow stale and taken-for-granted in the mouths of YHWH's omnivorous people. And YHWH can grow angry at our ingratitude and presumptuousness too. In the verses following today's appointed verses in Exodus we also encounter the interesting details that the Israelites were commanded by YHWH to gather only as much manna as they needed, for if more was gathered (as some greedy, less trusting Israelites soon discovered), any surplus gathered would be wormy and foul by morning (vv 16–23). Perhaps Jesus had this detail regarding manna in mind when he taught his disciples to pray, "*Give us this day our daily bread.*"

Jesus' discourse on the bread of life in John 6, which we'll be hearing for the next four Sundays, begins with his accosting the crowd for pursuing him across the Sea of Galilee not because of the "sign" he had performed in the feeding of the five thousand but simply because "*you ate your fill of the loaves,*" as Jesus himself says. Or, as we saw last week, at the conclusion of the story of the miraculous feeding, satisfying empty stomachs was sufficient for the people to want to "*take him by force to make him king*" (vv 26, 15)—Herod's worst nightmare! No wonder that Jesus then turns the occasion of his recent feeding of the crowd into a teaching moment as he urges them, "*Do not work for the food that perishes, but for the food that endures for eternal life, which the Son of Man will give you.*" And then to their plea for a sign Jesus offers the story of how YHWH provided the people with manna in the wilderness—*"bread from heaven to eat"* (vv 27, 31) which he reminds them came not through Moses but from God godself, who now offers them *"the true bread from heaven"* which *"gives life to the world."* To this they reply, *"Sir, give us this bread always,"* to which Jesus counters, sounding with his "I AM" more than a bit like YHWH from the burning bush, *"I am the bread of life. Whoever comes to me will never be hungry, and whoever believes in me will never thirst"* (vv 32–35).

Here the people's chronically self-serving, ingratitude-inflected question, "What's it?" becomes the sign, the occasion for Jesus' self-identification with the great "I AM" who is not only the world's creator but its continuing source of nurture and sustenance: the bread of life.

Taking it all a step further, our Ephesians text employs the metaphor of the body for the church which is nurtured and grows by the gift (food?) of God's love given in Christ Jesus. Moreover it is a unitive nourishment that God provides freely that issues in the seven-fold oneness that is the crowning affirmation of Ephesians, which has justly been called "the epistle of Christian unity": *"There is one body and one Spirit, just as you were called to the one hope of your calling, one Lord, one faith, one baptism, one God and Father of all, who is above all and through all and in all"* (vv 16, 4). Get it? One-ness in Christ.

Suitable hymns abound including the contemporary "Bread of Life from Heaven" (*ELW* #474), set to a traditional Argentinian hymn refrain with verses composed by Marty Haugen and words by Susan Briehl as well as "I Am the Bread of Life" (*ELW* #485) both of which can be repeated throughout the next several weeks. Or try "Lord, Who the Night You Were Betrayed" (*ELW* #463) whose refrain sings "may we all one bread, one body be, through this blest sacrament of unity."

Lectionary 19, Proper 14

Psalm 34:1–8
1 Kings 19:4–8
Ephesians 4:25—5:2
John 6:35, 41–51

O taste and see that the Lord is good;
happy are those who take refuge in him.

—Psalm 34:8

A Still, Small Voice

Among today's readings I'm especially drawn to one of my favorite stories in the OT that testifies so vividly to the "underwhelming" nature of God's presence among us. The larger context of today's story of God's self-disclosure to Elijah on the mountaintop takes us back to the previous chapter of 1 Kings in which Elijah's continuing confrontation with King Ahab and Queen Jezebel had culminated in the great "competition of the gods" on Mt. Carmel in which YHWH's sole, remaining prophet, Elijah, had stood up against the 450 prophets of the god Baal. You'll remember the scene, of how both Elijah and the prophets of Baal had sacrificed their own bulls and laid them on the wood of the altar and called on their respective deity to consume the sacrifices with fire. The story is told with an acute sense of humor evident in the details I can't go into here, but suffice it to say that Yahweh proves victorious, consuming the sacrifice with fire (*"holocaust"* is the Hebrew term), before Elijah, at YHWH's command, turns the holocaust in a human direction by slaying all of the prophets of Baal.

The immediate aftermath of this violent blood-letting is that the queen sent a messenger to Elijah threatening *"So may the gods do to me, and more also, if I do not make your life like the life of one of them* (meaning her slain prophets) *by this time tomorrow"* (19:2). And so Elijah, whom King Ahab had once called *"you troubler of Israel"* (18:18), like any sensible person, took off in fear of his life until finally we reach the beginning of today's appointed reading in which Elijah is found recovering from his exhausting flight into the wilderness, resting under the shade of a broom tree. Here he gives voice to not only his fear but also his frustration and sense of feeling sorry for himself that YHWH has not taken better care of his servant/prophet. *"It is enough,"* he whines. *"Now, O Lord, take away my life, for I am no better than my ancestors"* (19:4). Elijah, YHWH's mighty prophet, fresh upon his great victory over the prophets of Baal, celebrated by his blood-thirsty slaughter of his opponents, now inexplicably finds himself on the lam, in the depths of despair, wallowing in self-pity. I can't help but wonder what made Elijah think he was any better than his ancestors? At the very least it's a tip-off as to how full-of-himself he must have been after his stunning victory at Mt. Carmel.

This is only corroborated as the scene moves on as Elijah is revived by the touch of an angel who provides him with food and water and urges him on. Until he arrives at Mt. Horeb where the *"word of the Lord"* again confronts him and asks *"What are you doing here, Elijah?"*

Which is all the great prophet needs to hear to again lapse into a litany of self-justifying self-pity: *"I have been very zealous for the Lord, the God of hosts; for the Israelites have forsaken the covenant, thrown down your altars, and killed your prophets with the sword. I alone am left, and they are seeking my life, to take it away"* (vv 19:9–10). In other words he's whining, "God, I'm about all you've got left, and look how you're letting me be treated. Is this any way to reward your loyal servant?" I don't know about you, but there've been times in my ministry when I've felt this way as well, especially in those moments following some mountain-top experience that's been accompanied by a feeling of personal success and accomplishment and self-congratulation which all too soon is inevitably followed by the descent into the routine of everyday life with all its annoyances and problems. It's a common enough experience for us good, religious folks, I expect.

So what does YHWH do with his complaining, full-of-himself prophet but order him, *"Go out and stand on the mountain before the Lord, for the Lord is about to pass by."* Can you imagine Elijah's excitement at this promise of God's self-epiphany? The expected drama is only heightened as the text goes on to describe: *"Now there was a great wind, so strong that it was splitting mountain and breaking rocks in pieces before the Lord."* But the Lord was not in the wind nor the earthquake nor the fire that ensued, *"and after the fire a sound of sheer silence."* I like the assonance of the *NRSV* translation but it's difficult to improve on the *RSV*'s *"still, small voice."* Samuel Terrien sees this episode as a turning point in Hebrew scripture from God's making the divine presence known through "theophany" to that of the prophetic vision now become theophanic speech, what would become known as the "Word" of the Lord.[21]

    I remember the occasion like it was yesterday. I was serving as a counselor at a Bible camp and was growing tired of the unrelenting barrage of fire and brimstone we were encountering from an unusually conservative crew of "evangelical" preachers who seemed to have traded their good and gracious Lutheran theological training for conversionist, make-a-decision-for-Christ bombastics that I feared were misleading our young campers. Around the campfire one night I girded my loins and offered a simple prayer that we all might be able to hear the "still, small voice" of our loving and forgiving God amid all the unrelenting ranting and raving we were experiencing. Like Elijah I too survived the experience—and my own egoism—and was sent on my way to discern where God's call was leading me in life. As our Ephesians reading puts it *"let all of us speak the truth to our neighbors,"* remembering that *"we are members of one another"* (4:25). As we heard in last week's reading, let *"speaking the truth in love"* be the mark of our Christian maturity, of *"our grow*(ing) *up into him who is the head, into Christ . . . "* (v 15). While it's intended as a communion hymn, one of the few hymns extolling silence we have is the beautifully quiet verse "Now the Silence" by Jaroslav Vajda, *ELW* #460. Hymnwriters get busy!

Lectionary 20, Proper 15

Psalm 34:9–14
Proverbs 9:1–6
Ephesians 5:15–20
John 6:51–58

Come, O children, listen to me; I will teach you the fear of the Lord . . .
Depart from evil, and do good; seek peace, and pursue it.
—Psalm 34:11, 14

---

21. Terrien, *Elusive Presence* 230–236; see too my postil for Lectionary 19, Year A.

Year B

Wisdom's Feast

Today offers a rare opportunity to let the wisdom tradition within scripture take the lead as we hear the lovely lection from Proverbs 9 that is sometimes called "Wisdom's Feast." It invites us to hear our other readings from Ephesians and John 6 (and Psalm 34 also) with ears especially attuned to the ways in which the Word for today is being played in the key of wisdom, that minor strain of biblical literature that is chiefly thought of in terms of writings like Proverbs, Psalms, Ecclesiastes, Song of Solomon and Job. But wisdom is also at home in the New Testament in places like James and Ephesians and the Gospel of John, where Jesus is portrayed as the great teacher or rabbi whom we find declaring today, cryptically enough, "*I am the living bread that came down from heaven . . .* " (v 51). Rather than by means of "signs" as in John, in the synoptic Gospels Jesus characteristically teaches by means of riddling parables, using the most common, everyday things of life to evoke the secret of the kingdom of God.[22]

Wisdom, from a biblical perspective, is the fruit of reflection upon experience in the light of God's living Word—and so it is not a human accomplishment but is the gift of God's Spirit. Today's reading from Ephesians contains a good example of the "paranetic," advice-giving character of the Wisdom tradition: "*Be careful then how you live, not as unwise people but as wise, making the most of the time, because the days are evil. So do not be foolish* (the antonymn of wise) *but understand what the will of the Lord is. Do not get drunk with wine, for that is debauchery but be filled with the Spirit*" (vv 15–18)—the discerning Spirit of God's Wisdom. Wisdom is good advice raised to a higher degree, uncommonly good because godly sense.

One of the intriguing aspects of the figure of Wisdom as portrayed in scripture is that wisdom is not only a feminine noun but is portrayed as a woman—even as God's "consort" or "darling child" in a passage like Proverbs 8 in which Wisdom is "at once the delight of the creator and the companion of human beings" while also being "a member of the family of God," as Terrien puts it. The prologue to John's Gospel sounds itself like a wisdom hymn to the eternal Word with echoes of Proverbs' reference to preexistent Wisdom, "begotten not made."[23]

---

22. For a biblical theology especially appreciative of the wisdom tradition within scripture see Terrien's *Elusive God*.

23. Ibid., 356–357.

In today's brief reading from Proverbs 9, Wisdom is portrayed as an enthusiastic hostess, who has carefully set her table, planned and prepared her multi-coursed meal, chosen and decanted her wine all in readiness to welcome guests to her table. Who are the guests? To the task of figuring this out she delegates her servant girls who are sent out into the town with the open invitation, "*You that are simple, turn in here!*" and to those without sense "*Come, eat of my bread and drink of the wine I have mixed. Lay aside immaturity, and live, and walk in the way of insight*" (vv 2–6). It is a metaphor, an image, after all, that Proverbs is offering us that we too—simple and without sense as we may be—are especially welcomed to Wisdom's feast.

Christians cannot hear of Wisdom's feast, of course, without thinking of Jesus, his characteristic table fellowship with the religiously excluded, his feeding of the five thousand, his parable of the great banquet, and his final meal with his friends, which the church would commemorate ever after as its central act of worship at Jesus' command. Around the table we trust Jesus' words—as in today's Gospel reading—that in this simple meal of bread and wine, a true eating and drinking of Jesus' own body and blood is being experienced in which the original host himself becomes the meal—the living bread come down from heaven. It is not hard to imagine that Wisdom's feast from Proverbs 9 may well have been one of Jesus' favorite passages from his people's scriptures.

The first parish I served as pastor had a non-communing member named Elo who never came to worship but came to every other sort of eating opportunity we hosted—monthly birthday dinners, Thanksgiving feasts, pot-lucks, senior citizen lunches, you name it. I once asked him, "Elo, why is it you come to nearly every eating opportunity we offer but never come to church for worship?" He looked at me with a sparkle in his eye and said: "I'm just an eating member of the church." Well, that didn't fully answer my question or my concern for Elo's spiritual well-being—I wanted him to feel welcome at the Lord's table as well as at all those other tables. But I smiled and nodded my head that, yes indeed, there is a sense in which we're all just eating members of the church—and maybe, just maybe, Elo had a more comprehensive idea of holy communion than I did.

"*Turn in here*"—Wisdom's invitation to her banquet—also might be taken up by the church generally as our invitation to others to "*come and see*" what it is that is on offer here. And thanks to Ephesians we're told that this matter of being filled with the Spirit of Wisdom has certain outcomes of which one is music, or if you will, participatory song. *"Be filled with the Spirit,"* our reading from Ephesians closes, *"as you sing psalms and hymns and spiritual songs among yourselves, singing and making melody to the Lord in your hearts, giving thanks to God the Father at all times and for everything in the name of our Lord Jesus Christ"* (vv 18b–20). "All God's Critters Got a Place in the Choir" is part of the church's invitation as well, creating the participatory dinner music essential to truly eucharistic worship. Try the newish hymn, "We Eat the Bread of Teaching" (*ELW* #518) which sings of how "Wisdom calls throughout the city,/knows our hunger, and in pity/ gives her loving invitation/to the banquet of salvation."

Lectionary 21, Proper 16

Psalm 34:15–22
Joshua 24:1–2a, 14–18
Ephesians 6:10–20
John 6:56–69

The Lord is near to the broken-hearted, and saves the crushed in spirit.

—Psalm 34:18

"Do You Also Wish to Go Away?"

For five weeks now we've been working our way through the sixth chapter of John's Gospel that consists chiefly of Jesus' l-o-n-g soliloquy on what it means for him to claim *"I am the bread of life."* Today Jesus ends his sermon—as all sermons must finally end—and it's at least reassuring to us preacher-types that even Jesus' sermons didn't always receive a polite and positive hearing.

In fact, John reports, *"When many of his disciples heard it, they said, 'This teaching is difficult; who can accept it?'"* (v 60). The Greek word translated as "difficult" is *"skleros"*—like "sclerosis" in English—but in Greek it can also mean "dry" as well as "hard." Its connotations also include, my lexicon tells me, "harsh" or "rough," "stiff" or "stark," "austere" or "stern." "Too tough to swallow," I'd translate it. "Difficult" is just too wishy-washy. "A rough, crude teaching. Who wants to hear that?" I imagine his disciples saying. And yes, please notice that it's his disciples—not the crowd, nor the scribes, nor the Pharisees—but his own followers and friends who find Jesus' teaching about the bread of life, and especially about the need for them to *"eat my flesh and drink my blood"* (v 56) too hard to swallow (oops, forgive the pun). I remember years ago an older, much respected pastor, objecting to what he thought the too graphic words of the then contemporary hymn which sang in its refrain "Eat my body, drink my blood." The words still have the power to offend the faithful.

But Jesus, being a good teacher and not insensible to the cool reception his sermon had received, asks his disciples (I like to think, with a slight smile creasing his face), *"Does this offend you?"* (v 61). Again, a weak translation, for the Greek literally says, "Does this scandalize you? Do you find this a stumbling block?" Indeed it must have, for John bothers to tell us that *"many of his disciples turned back and no longer went about with him"* (v 66). This matter of eating his flesh and drinking his blood was apparently the straw that broke the camel's back for some who had counted themselves among his followers. So Jesus turned to the twelve, the inner circle among his disciples, and asks them with what one commentator calls "unsettling directness": *"Do you also wish to go away?"* (v 67).

I imagine Jesus asking the question sadly, sighing as his shoulders sagged a little, as he saw one-time followers in whom he'd invested a great deal of himself shaking their heads in disbelief or dissatisfaction or whatever it is that disillusions folks who'd once evidenced excitement and commitment. I've seen it in church members who get mad or frustrated about something or at someone and threaten to leave, or just stop coming and won't even make the effort to explain why. Jesus' question, *"So you also want to go away?"*, makes him sound almost pathetic, doesn't it?

But, to be honest, I've got to admit that there are times when I myself have been tempted to answer "Yep" to Jesus' question. Yep, I've had it with this church business—enough prejudice, enough injustice, enough hardheadedness, enough stinginess, enough guilt over my own inadequacies or mistakes, enough seemingly endless church meetings—like when our Synod Assembly couldn't even manage to pass a resolution against torture!

"*Do you also wish to go away?*" Jesus asks. But the question isn't one Jesus invented. It really goes back to Adam and Eve in the Garden and, as Jesus himself suggests in John 6, is epitomized in Israel's wilderness wanderings only made possible by YHWH's life-sustaining gift of manna—about which the Israelites incessantly complained—culminating in today's climactic story from the Book of Joshua. "*Choose this day whom you will serve,*" Joshua urges the people at a critical juncture in their history but "*as for me and my household, we will serve the Lord*" (v 15). "You gotta' serve somebody," Bob Dylan taught us to sing during his all-too-brief evangelical phase. "It may be the devil or it may be the Lord, but you gotta' serve somebody." But Israel's well-meaning if sanctimonious opting for YHWH, "*Far be it from us that we should forsake the Lord to serve other gods*" (v 16), once again reveals that our human choosing is never the final word, however good the intentions. Only God's choosing to remain loyal to the covenant promises is finally what matters, hard as the prophets will try to remind Israel and us of our covenantal obligations.

It's, as so often, Simon Peter who steps forward to answer Jesus' question, "*Do you also wish to go away?*" with the words we join him in singing weekly as our Gospel acclamation, "*Lord, to whom can we go? You have the words of eternal life. We have come to believe and know that you are the Holy One of God*" (vv 68–69). As our reading from Ephesians reminds us, "*our struggle is not against enemies of blood and flesh, but against the rulers, against the authorities, against the cosmic powers of this present darkness, against the spiritual forces of evil in the heavenly places*" (v 12).

For all the bravado of Ephesians' image of our being clad in "*the whole armor of God*" from head to foot, with its allegorical array of defensive weapons deployed against "*that evil day*" (v 13–17), I've long found the transfigured military image imbedded in Bonhoeffer's late prison poem "Who Am I?" far more compelling because rooted in Jesus' hard saying of what it means to participate in his body and blood: ". . . is something within me still like a beaten army, fleeing in disorder from victory already achieved? Who am I? They mock me, these lonely questions of mine. Whoever I am, thou knowest, O God, I am thine."[24] You could do worse than sing Bonhoeffer's hymn, "By Gracious Powers" (*ELW* #626). "I Am the Bread of Life" (*ELW* #485) is one of very few communion hymns to speak directly of our eating of Christ's flesh and drinking of his body in the sacrament in close paraphrase of today's Gospel text.

24. Bonhoeffer, *Letters and Papers* 189.

Lectionary 22, Proper 17

Psalm 15
Deuteronomy 4:1–2, 6–9
James 1:17–27
Mark 7:1–8, 14–15, 21–23

O Lord, who may abide in your tent?
Who may dwell on your holy hill?
Those who walk blamelessly, and do what is right,
and speak the truth from their heart.

—Psalm 15:1–2

Poets of the Word

Labor Day is not only the national holiday that we in the US use to mark the end of summer, highlighted by the beginning of school and college students' migration back to campus. Traditionally it's a day devoted to the celebration of work—that everyday reality of life by which, as we say, we earn our daily bread. And yet, of course, from a Christian perspective, labor is an important part of our larger, everyday "calling" or "vocation" from God. As Brother Martin reminded the late medieval church of his day, no work is more inherently Christian, more God-pleasing, than any other—least of all, perhaps, professional "religious" work.

Our scripture readings for today (finally, moved back from our recent forays into Ephesians and John to the Letter of James and the Gospel according to St. Mark), warn us of a particular danger to which we human beings are particularly susceptible: the temptation that Paul and Martin Luther after him identified as "works righteousness," the illusion that we can work our way into God's favor by doing certain good deeds and adopting particular religious behaviors.

Jesus encounters this attitude on the part of the Pharisees and scribes in today's Gospel reading who are quick to criticize Jesus and his disciples for not keeping scrupulously enough—and for therefore violating—the religious traditions of their day and particularly the purity laws of his people. Jesus, in turn, critiques the religiously fastidious of his day for elevating human religious traditions that sought to "hedge" the law—keeping the "letter of the law" sancrosanct—over the "spirit of the law," which is God's good gift to Israel. Jesus counter-charges, citing the prophet Isaiah who had six hundred years earlier declared on YHWH's behalf: *"This people honors me with their lips, but their hearts are far from me; in vain do they worship me, teaching human precepts as doctrines . . . ."* In sum, Jesus charges, *"You abandon the commandment of God and hold to human tradition"* (v 6–8). While not at all disparaging the law, Jesus maintains that *"there is nothing outside a person that by going in can defile, but the things that come out are what defile"* (v 14). External behaviors are only the expression of inner dispositions.

In our reading from the Letter of James from which our second readings will be taken throughout this coming month, we find a collection of what I like to think of as good, common-sense Christian advice, a piece of the early church's wisdom literature that was written out of a strongly Jewish-Christian context, attributed traditionally to James, the brother of Jesus and head of the church gathered in Jerusalem. While probably not written by James himself, its strongly Jewish-Christian content offers us a glimpse of the early church as it struggled to define itself as the Jesus movement among a variety of contending Jewish sectarian movements of the day amid an even more pluralistic Hellenistic culture governed by Rome itself and its many cults including that of the emperor. September would be a good opportunity to lead a Bible study of James, especially in light of its poor reputation among followers of Luther, Brother Martin once notoriously having referred to James as "an epistle of straw." William F. Brosend II's *James and Jude* is a good resource for an adult study and commentary.

With Jesus, James agrees that one's behavior is determined by one's inner state and not by religious regulations. James speaks of how *"every generous act of giving, with every perfect gift is from above, coming down from the Father of lights . . ."* who, in quasi-baptismal language, *"gave us birth by the word of truth, so that we would become the first fruits of his creation."* Nonetheless, James insists that we be *"doers of the word, and not merely hearers who deceive themselves,"* not *"hearers who forget but doers who act,"* and that we do so by looking into the *"mirror"* of the *"perfect law, the law of liberty"* (17–18, 22–25). It's Luther himself who once called the

Ten Commandments the "*Sachsenspiegel*" of the Jews, meaning the "looking glass" of the Saxons, the mirror of their own behavior in which every people is revealed for what they really are, one of the true purposes of God's law. As we'll see further in next week's reading from James, his concern is that faith, by itself, "*if it has no works is dead*" (2:17)—that faith must be active in love in order to be true faith.

I like to point out that in urging his readers to be "*doers of the word and not hearers only*" James is using the Greek word "*poietes*" which we translate rather prosaicly as "doers" but which, in fact, is the same Greek word from which our English word "poet" derives. This suggests to me that the "doing of the word" James is calling us to, rather than being merely "hearers" is a creative, active and even poetic, response to God's "implanted" Word in our daily lives in which we are called to love our neighbor, literally being "poets of the Word," imaginative agents of God's Word in our world.

Lest we become too airy-fairy in our call to be doers of the word, James reminds us in today's closing words that being "religious" is worthless if it does not begin with something as plain and simple as "*to care for orphans and widows in their distress*" (v 27). As Jesus in Luke 10 will remind us, *the* question is not one of figuring out "who is my neighbor" but rather in being a neighbor to the one in need whom we encounter in our daily life. "True religion," in James' understanding, is not the ancient equivalent of complicated rocket science—it's taking action in the face of genuine human need. That's what's behind all the "*statutes and ordinances*" given Israel as God's good gift which in the observance (and certainly not in the breach) will show Israel's "*wisdom and discernment*" and lead other peoples to say of Israel, YHWH's specially chosen, "*Surely this great nation is a wise and discerning people*" (Deut 4:1–6). Try "Come to Us, Creative Spirit" (*ELW* #687) as your hymn of the day which sings in verse two "Poet, painter, music maker, all your treasures bring;/ craftsman, actor, graceful dancer, make your offering;/ join your hands in celebration: let creation shout and sing!"

Year B

Lectionary 23, Proper 18

Psalm 146
Isaiah 35:4–7a
James 2:1–10 [11–13] 14–17
Mark 7:24–37

> *Happy are those whose help is the God of Jacob,*
> *whose hope is in the Lord their God,*
> *who made heaven and earth, the sea, and*
> *all that is in them; who keeps faith forever;*
> *who executes justice for the oppressed;*
> *who gives food to the hungry.*
>
> —PSALM 146:5–7

Faith That Works

Last week we encountered Jesus "unloading" in uncharacteristically harsh fashion on the Pharisees, that party within Judaism of his day that prided itself upon its minute observance of torah. In no uncertain terms Jesus condemned the puritanical and exclusive elements of Pharisaic teaching that aimed at an ideal of ritual purity that would keep Israel untainted by the immorality and uncleanness of her pagan, gentile neighbors. Today in the very next story Mark tells we hear of Jesus wandering into foreign, gentile territory, the region of Tyre and ancient home of the sea-faring Phoenician peoples who produced our alphabet

A curious spin in Mark's telling of the tale is that Jesus "*did not want anyone to know that he was there*," and the absence of mention of the disciples suggests that Jesus may have gotten away from them for a time, for a little "r and r" perhaps, after his confrontation with the scribes and Pharisees and crowd he had just left. At any rate, the text says, "*he could not escape notice*," perhaps as a Jew in gentile territory and he's immediately accosted by a woman of "Syrophoenecian origin," as Mark takes care to tell us, who begins to beg Jesus to cast an unclean spirit, also called a "demon," out of her little daughter. See my comments in the postil for Year A, Lectionary 20, which deals at length with Jesus' seemingly harsh conversation with the woman—which I take to be a kind of bantering repartee—in which she seems to emerge victorious in the word-play as well as in getting Jesus to exorcize her daughter of the evil spirit. The whole encounter, is a "dirty, unclean" affair, from the Pharisaic perspective, for any law-abiding Jewish man to have conversation with a gentile woman was out of bounds.

This episode is followed immediately by Jesus' reported healing of a deaf man with a speech impediment, on his way back to the Sea of Galilee, in the region of the Decapolis. Here Jesus' healing includes the curious details of his putting his fingers into the man's ears, his spitting and touching the man's tongue, and then looking up to heaven and uttering the word "*ephphatha*," which Mark bothers to tell us means "*be opened*". "*And immediately his ears were opened, his tongue was released, and he spoke plainly. Then Jesus ordered them to tell no one, but the more he ordered them the more zealously they proclaimed it,*" (vv 31–36). Apparently Jesus' authority didn't include the power to make the crowd bite their collective tongue, but our first reading from Isaiah reminds us of the prophetic promise of just such a time when "*the eyes of the blind shall be opened, and the ears of the deaf unstopped*" (v 5) which we also hear as our appointed reading for Advent 3 in Year A.

The "insiders/outsiders" theme is interestingly paralleled in today's lection from the Letter of James which begins with this very practical but withering question which, while nineteen hundred years old, is as fresh as today: "*My brothers and sisters, do you with your acts of favoritism really believe in our Lord Jesus Christ?*" And James gets uncomfortably specific, "*For if a person with gold rings and in fine clothes comes into your assembly and if a poor person in dirty clothes also comes in, and if you take notice of the one wearing the fine clothes say, 'Have a seat here, please,' while to the one who is poor you say, 'Stand there' or 'Sit at my feet,' have you not made distinctions among yourselves and become judges with evil thoughts?*" (vv 1–3). Who of us hasn't shown favoritism in treating some folks better than others, often merely on the basis of appearance? But James isn't done. "*Listen, my beloved brothers and sisters, has not God chosen the poor in the world to be rich in faith and to be heirs of the dominion promised to those who love God?*" Wasn't this exactly James' brother's Jesus point when he declared so memorably in his beatitudes, "*Blessed are the poor, theirs is the dominion of heaven?*" Isn't this just what the Latin American bishops more than a generation ago meant by coining the term "God's preferential option for the poor," which Pope Francis seems so intent on reviving in our day?

But James goes on to sharpen his point still further (in a "socialist" direction fueling the flames of "class war" some Christians would claim in our day): "*Is it not the rich who oppress you? Is it not they who drag you into court? Is it not they who blaspheme the excellent name that was invoked over you?*" (vv 6–7). Important questions for the faith community now as then in an age that glamorizes the "rich and famous" and idolizes the so-called "free market" and its trickle-down economics—the "crumbs from the table" theory of distribution, we might call it from Jesus' confrontation with the Syrophoenician woman. James saw the rich as the problem, not the solution, of the gap between rich and poor. It's not that "*acts of favoritism*" aren't appropriate in church. It's who's being favored that's the problem.

All of this is brought to a crowning point as James quotes his brother Jesus who himself was quoting the words of torah in what James wondrously nicknames "*the royal law*": "*You shall love your neighbor as yourself.*" I keep wondering why the fuss about posting the Ten Commandments in our courthouses and schools. Why not advocate instead for the posting of the non-sectarian command: "*love your neighbor as yourself?*" And James clinches his point by suggesting yet another adage that is worth posting wherever our criminal justice system purports to do its difficult work: "*Mercy triumphs over judgment*" (vv 8, 13b).

The conclusion to today's reading takes us back to what we heard James telling us last week when he urged us to "*be doers of the word and not hearers only*" as he takes up an issue in the church of his day that may have been the result of a misperception of the apostle Paul's diatribe against works righteousness, later so important to Martin Luther and the church of his day. "*What good is it, my brothers and sisters, if you say you have faith but do not have works? Can faith save you*"? (v 14). Well, can faith save you— faith without works? To get specific, as James always likes to do, he offers a further case in point. "*If a brother or sister is naked and lacks daily food, and one of your says to them, 'Go in peace; keep warm and eat your fill,' and yet do not supply their bodily needs, what is the good of that?*" (vv 15–16). Can a "have a nice day" or even a benediction feed a hungry stomach?

James answers his own rhetorical question and brother Martin and all good Lutherans will have to agree: "*faith by itself, if it has no works, is dead*" (v 17). Faith simply is "active in love," was Luther's way of putting it—or it isn't faith in the first place. Real faith flowers forth in the fruits of love of neighbor. No, good works don't merit God's approval, good works don't produce faith, nor from a Lutheran standpoint even "cooperate" with God's grace (see here, for example, the Lutheran/Roman Catholic *Joint Declaration on the Doctrine of Justification* of 1999). But faith without works is dead, deadening, and deathly. A lovely Spanish language hymn most fitting for today is "When the Poor Ones" (*ELW* #725) as is the Reformation era "Salvation Unto Us Has Come" (*ELW* #590) which sings "For faith alone can justify;/works serve our neighbor and supply/the proof that faith is living" (v 3).

Lectionary 24, Proper 19

Psalm 116:1–9
Isaiah 50:4–9a
James 3:1–12
Mark 8:27–38

Gracious is the Lord, and righteous; our God is merciful.
The Lord protects the simple...

—PSALM 116:5–6A

A Tongue-lashing

It was two weeks ago that we heard James begin his Letter with the admonition, *"Be quick to listen, slow to speak"* (1:19) and today we find him returning to this topic by dwelling on the ambivalent character of the tongue—which I hope you'll notice is precisely what got Simon Peter into trouble in today's Gospel reading, his penchant for "shooting from the hip," as we say, and blurting out whatever he was thinking. Today, in return, he receives from Jesus an uncharacteristic tongue-lashing (pun intended) in which the future pope is called "satan," meaning "a hinderer of God." We have to admire Peter's *chutzpah,* daring to instruct Jesus on how the true Messiah is supposed to act. And yet again we find Peter putting his foot in his mouth, as we say. Which leads me to speculate that maybe it was Peter who first came to mind as James penned his advice, *"Be quick to listen, slow to speak."*

Which reminds me of an old *"Peanuts"* cartoon in which Lucy is out for a stroll with Marcy, carrying on, as is normal for Lucy, a conversation largely with herself, musing about the upcoming Christmas pageant. Lucy begins by enthusing, "I'm going to ask the teacher if I can be Mary in the Christmas play this year." To which Marcy quietly and respectfully objects, "But she's already asked me, sir." But Lucy, already deep in her reverie about playing the starring role, hasn't heard a word and with a far-away glint in her eye murmurs, "I think I'll be great in the part," to which Marcy reiterates doggedly, "She asked *me* yesterday." But by now Lucy is off and running in her private dream-world and says: "I like the part where the angel Gabriel talks to me." But by now Marcy's heard enough, stops dead in her tracks, dumbfounded and blurts out, "But why would Gabriel talk to you? You never listen!" Which, if you know Lucy, is probably the truest thing ever said of her. The strip ends with Lucy looking admiringly at her own upraised foot, saying, "I can probably wear these same sandals."

"You never listen!" Marcy says to Lucy. And James says, "Let everyone be quick to listen, slow to speak." James' brother, Jesus' way of putting it was *"Let anyone with ears to hear, listen!"* (Mark 4:9, 4:23 and elsewhere in the synoptics), one of his widest-attested sayings.

Perhaps James had the words of the prophet Isaiah in mind, words we hear as our first reading every Palm/Passion Sunday, which I like to think of as encouragement to open our ears and practice deep listening to the passion story we're about to hear and re-live throughout the ensuing days of Holy Week. The lection from Isaiah begins, *"The Lord God has given me the tongue of a teacher, that I may know how to sustain the weary with a word. Morning by morning he wakens —wakens my ear to listen as those who are taught. The Lord God has opened my ear . . . "* (vv 4–5a). James, like Isaiah, links his warning about the danger of the tongue with the gift of listening to the calling of teachers: *"Not many of you should become teachers, my brothers and sisters, for you know that we who teach will be judged with greater strictness."* And then James adds, almost as an afterthought, what has become one of my favorite verses in scripture, one I relish using out of context, since it's so universally applicable: *"For all of us make many mistakes*." Now isn't that the gospel truth!? All of us, indeed, make mistakes. No, all of us make *many* mistakes, which James immediately follows with the seeming tautology, "*Anyone who makes no mistakes in speaking is perfect*" (vv 1–2). Have any of us ever met such a person? Even and especially while gazing into a mirror?

But now James is off and running, on a free-wheeling word association sort of riff on the dangers of the tongue, that "*small member*" which is the source of both "*blessing and cursing*" but which "*is placed among our members as a world of iniquity; it stains the whole body, sets on first the cycle of nature, and is itself set on fire by hell.*" Every species can be tamed, James claims in a bit of an overstatement perhaps, but not the human tongue, "*a restless evil, full of deadly poison.*" Bits and bridles can control the horse, and a small rudder a large ship, but who can control the tongue which is a "fire" (vv 3–6).? Whew! Who knows what tongue-lashings James may have endured to lead him to such a rant, but he uses all his rhetorical ingenuity to let us see the dangers of a "loose tongue."[25]

Following the fireworks of Peter's confession of Jesus as Messiah and his evident refusal to accept the implications of what this would mean in terms of Jesus' impending passion and death, Jesus calls together his disciples along with the crowd and lays out for them his theology of the cross, which involves their taking up their own crosses and being willing to lose their lives for Jesus' sake and the Gospel's in order to save them. This letting go evidently has something to do with the counter-cultural behavior of biting one's tongue and opening one's ears. "Listen, God is Calling" (*ELW* #513), a lively song from Tanzania, is the first hymn that comes to mind although it would be a good exercise in liturgical irony to sing the old Wesley song "O For a Thousand Tongues to Sing" (*ELW* #886).

---

25. For a contemporary, secular counterpart to James' disquisition on the wisdom of listening over talking see Cain's recent best-seller *Quiet* subtitled *The Power of Introverts in a World that Can't Stop Talking*.

Year B

Lectionary 25, Proper 20

Psalm 54
Jeremiah 11:18–20 or Wisdom 1:16—2:1, 12–22
James 3:13—4:3, 7–8a
Mark 9:30–37

*Save me O God, by your name, and vindicate me by your might.
Hear my prayer O God; give ear to the words of my mouth.*

—Psalm 54:1–2

Being #1

Wouldn't you know that in the very wake of Jesus' second passion prediction, much like the first we heard last week, prophesying his own betrayal and killing and resurrection, the topic of conversation among his disciples as they passed through Galilee on their way back to Capernaum would be an argument as to which of them was the greatest? Greatest at what, in what, or for what we're not told—just who's the greatest. And not, I expect, for the first or, as we'll see in the Gospel reading a few weeks from now, for the last time. At least to Jesus' question as to what they were arguing about along the way they had the good sense to be silent, sensing, I expect, that they knew that Jesus wouldn't approve of such a topic of conversation.

Instead of reproving the disciples (perhaps word had leaked out from the inner circle of Jesus' transfiguration on the mountaintop prompting a sudden interest in the topic of who'd have preference in the promised and imminent kingdom of God), Jesus simply sits the twelve down for a little object lesson and utters a gospel adage we'll be hearing again that is a sort of corollary of his recent admonition heard last week that following him involved taking up one's own cross and letting go of one's life in order to save it. Here Jesus simply says, *"Whoever wants to be first must be last of all and servant of all."* And to seal his point in a kind of real-life parable, he took a little child which he first set in their midst without saying a word, then lifted it up in his arms and said to them, *"Whoever welcomes one such child in my name welcomes me, and whoever welcomes me welcomes not me but the one who sent me"* (vv 30–37). In a flash, an embarrassing and extremely inappropriate argument becomes a teaching moment regarding the topsy-turvy values of the kingdom of God. A little child, literally a non-person in ancient estimation of social privilege and preference, is given first place by Jesus and being hospitable to such a seeming contradiction to the normal way of the world is declared by Jesus to be an act of welcome to *"the one who sent me."* The Gospel of the Lord!

Our reading from James serves as a kind of ancient sapiential pscho-analysis of the disciples' wrangling over greatness. *"Those conflicts and disputes among you, where do they come from?"* James asks, almost as if he were commenting upon today's Gospel reading. The question isn't meant to be rhetorical for James immediately answers with his own question, *"Do they not come from your cravings that are at war within you?"* For example, getting specific, as James likes to be, he suggests, *"You want something and do not have it; so you commit murder. And you covet something and cannot obtain it; so you engage in disputes and conflicts"* (4:1–2). There you have it—an application of Jesus' words from a couple of weeks ago regarding how all of our behavior is determined by what comes out of us from within, from our internal disposition, not from external rules and regulations. Sounding like an ancient Dr. Phil, James says that it all begins as an internal matter of *"bitter envy and selfish ambition in your hearts"* (3:14).

And so, James says, it is the mark of wisdom and understanding to *"show by your good life that your works are done with gentleness born of wisdom,"* which sounds to me, along with the *"implanted word"* of which we heard a couple of weeks ago, like baptismal language. There is another kind of wisdom, however, which *"does not come down from above, but is earthly, unspiritual, devilish."* As always James is eager to give particulars, *"for where there is envy and selfish ambition"* (again, think of the disciples and their argument along the way to Capernaum) *"there will also be disorder and wickedness of every kind"* (3:13, 15–16).

But James also wants to get explicit about the fruits of heavenly wisdom and goes on to catalogue a full seven adjectives that identify the *"wisdom from above."* They are: *"first pure, then peaceable, gentle, willing to yield, full of mercy and good fruits, without a trace of partiality or hypocrisy"* (3:17–18). I've sometimes in my sermons on this text taken the time to focus on these seven, highly descriptive Greek adjectives that James uses here, suggesting that together they constitute something very like how the "life style" of Jesus himself might be described. *"Agnos"* means "pure" but also "holy" or my favorite translation, "innocent." *"Eirenike"* means "peaceful" as translated, or "irenic," a word we still use in English. It means not only serene and tranquil but "peace-creating" with the rich and beautiful connotations of the Hebrew word "shalom" as in Jesus' blessing of what he calls the "peacemakers" in his beatitudes.

The *"wisdom from above"* is next *"epiekes,"* James says, a word one biblical scholar has called "of all Greek words in the New Testament the most untranslatable." It's a word that the Greek philosopher Aristotle once defined as meaning "beyond the written law." It describes one who knows how to temper justice with mercy, reminding us of James' adage mentioned earlier of how *"mercy triumphs over justice."* The NRSV translates it as *"gentle."* Next is the adjective *"eupeithes,"* another difficult-to-translate word which the NRSV prefers to translate as *"willing to yield"* over the RSV's earlier "open to reason." I prefer something like "willing to give in" or, in light of last week's reading from James, "willing to listen," the quality that Paul counsels the Corinthian church to adopt that "does not insist on its own way."

Fifthly, the *"wisdom from above"* is *"meste eleous kai karpon agathon,"* a phrase meaning "filled to brimming over with mercy and good fruits," the "good fruits" of "faith active in love," the fruits that demonstrate the authenticity of true faith, according to James. And finally James gives us two related words that are negatively stated—*"adiachritos"* and *"anhupokritos"*—words translated in the NRSV as "without a trace of partiality or hypocrisy." To put it more positively in English they mean simply "straight-forward and sincere," the latter word literally meaning "unhypocritical." (vv 15–18).

This, James says, is the impact of the wisdom from above, the antidote to violence and the aggressive lust for power and ambition to be number #1 that simmers within us. This is the Spirit's baptismal gift which it is promised drowns the "old Adam and Eve" within us and waters the fruits of faith which mature into the good works of love done on behalf of our neighbor. And James' promise is that thereby *"a harvest of righteousness is sown in peace for those who make peace"* (v 18). The gift of the *"wisdom from above,"* James seems to be saying, brings with it its own reward. Try the newish hymn "We Eat the Bread of Teaching" (*ELW* #518), a lovely if simple hymn that sings of how "Wisdom calls throughout the city" extending her "loving invitation to the banquet of salvation."

Lectionary 26, Proper 21

Psalm 19:7–14
Numbers 11:4–6, 10–16, 24–29
James 5:13–20
Mark 9:38–50

*Let the words of my mouth and the
meditation of my heart be acceptable to you,
O Lord, my rock and my redeemer.*

—PSALM 19:14

Tattle-Tales

Jesus' disciples haven't been looking too good these last few weeks in our Gospel readings. Last week we found Jesus catching them arguing about who's the greatest, the week before that Jesus found it necessary to rebuke Peter, even telling the future pope, in effect, "go to hell, Satan, where you belong!" Next week we'll find the disciples playing hard guys with a bunch of kids who'd come to see Jesus and then, again, several weeks from now we'll encounter a couple of Jesus' inner circle of disciples arguing over preferential seating at Jesus' right or left hand in the kingdom. They just don't seem to get it, do they, the nature of this kingdom whose presence Jesus is always preaching as being so near? I often marvel at how all these stories that make the disciples look so bad ever made the cut into the Bible. "Apostolic succession" indeed! It's not so much the laying on of the hands of bishops throughout the ages from the time of these original apostles that is the heart of the tradition of the church's leadership as it is the sheer hard-headedness, the downright cussedness, of Jesus' own followers from then until now—from them down to us!

Today we find one of the disciples, John, stepping forward like some little tattle-tale running to the teacher from the playground (and you have to get the whining tone of voice just right), "Teeeecher—*we saw someone* casting out demons in your name and we tried to stop him because he was not following us" (v 38). Did you get those pronouns? "*We tried to stop him because he was not following us.*" Well, I thought being a disciple meant to be a follower of Jesus, but here already before their master's crucifixion and resurrection the disciples are expecting someone to follow them! It's too funny and too sad and too true. Like some wit once put it, "Jesus taught us to pray for the coming of the kingdom, and what did we get but the church?" It might help to know that a few verses earlier Mark had told the story of how Jesus had exorcized a young boy of seizures which were believed to have been caused by an unclean spirit. Following the healing the disciples came "*privately*" to Jesus to ask "*Why couldn't we cast it out?*" "*This kind can come out only through prayer,*" (vv 28–29), Jesus answers, implying that the disciples were already, you see, a little sensitive on this particular topic of healing and didn't appreciate some other guy they didn't even know healing in Jesus' name—and maybe praying with more effect than they could. All of which leads up to Jesus' great punch-line in today's text, one we need to hear again and again: "*Whoever is not against us is for us*" (v 40). It's an aphorism from Jesus' lips that might have some particular relevance in a pluralistic age and setting like our own, amid a political climate that finds it hard to live positively with diversity and is suspicious of those not known to be "true believers."

Then follows a spate of sharp words of Jesus, hard, edgy words that may well seem to us to be uncharacteristic of "gentle Jesus, meek and mild"—words reeking of hellfire and brimstone in which Jesus even seems to be recommending self-mutilation as a preventative to sin. And, of course, there have always been crazy literalists who can't take a joke, or rather, can't detect hyperbole when they hear it, can't imagine Jesus taking a little liberty in his language with his witless disciples. Please notice that here Jesus isn't addressing the crowd or the scribes and Pharisees but his own disciples whom he wants to impress with the utter seriousness of offending, of causing to "trip up," any of the "*little ones who believe in me*" (v 42). And for Jesus, as always, the disciples' typically excluding behavior is what such scandalous offense usually consists of—excluding children, excluding gentiles, excluding those looking for healing.

But there's yet another tattle-tale story heard in today's readings, this from the time of Israel's wilderness wanderings, and, as I warned some weeks ago, yet another account that begins with Israel's chronic lament about the manna ("what's it?") they had to eat and their longing for what they remember as the scrumptious food they used to eat in Egypt in the good ol' days of slavery. Moses here has had it with their grumbling and takes it out on YHWH who has laid this *"burden"* on him. It would be funny if it weren't so serious (it's still humorously told), as Moses grumbles to YHWH, *"Did I conceive all this people? Did I give birth to them, that you should say to me, 'Carry them in your bosom, as a nurse carries a suckling child.' Where am I to get meat to give to all these people?"* (vv 12–13). Amazing, isn't it, that such irreverent dialogue should find its way into the Bible, picturing the revered Moses as a put-upon Jewish mother. I'd love to see Larry David play the part.

But even more amazing is that YHWH listens to Moses' complaint and goes to its heart by devising a new plan whereby the leadership that Moses feels to be so burdensome is "democratized," to use an anachronistic Greek word. And so seventy of the elders are gathered at YHWH's direction in the tent of meeting and some of the spirit given Moses by God was allotted to the seventy. But that's not the end of it. Wouldn't you know that two men, with the hilarious names of Eldad and Medad, weren't there with the seventy but ended up prophesying like the others anyway as if they too had been given a portion of YHWH's spirit shared with the seventy (which somehow they had received, the story says). And so none other than Joshua, soon to be named Moses' successor, tattles on them to Moses, pleading, *"My lord Moses, stop them!"* But Moses has the good sense to ask Joshua, *"Are you jealous for my sake? Would that all the Lord's people were prophets, and that the Lord would put his spirit on them!"* (vv 16–29). I guess a good story is worth re-telling. Servant-leadership seems always to have been a hard lesson for God's people to learn. Some say it still is. "Rise Up, O Saints of God" (*ELW* #669) with its line "From vain ambitions turn" is a possible choice for hymn but try too the newer "Will You Let Me Be Your Servant?" (*ELW* #659) from the Iona community.

Year B

Lectionary 27, Proper 22

Psalm 8
Genesis 2:18–24
Hebrews 1:1–4; 2:5–12
Mark 10:2–16

*When I look at your heavens . . . the moon
and the stars that you have established;
what are human beings that you are mindful
of them, mortals that you care for them?*

—Psalm 8:3–4

Not Good!

Today we move from several weeks of hearing from the Epistle of James as our second reading to a perhaps equally as neglected New Testament book, the Letter to the Hebrews, from which we'll be reading until the last Sunday of the church year, some seven Sundays in all. This would be a good opportunity to lead a Bible study on this rather difficult, and along with James, one of the most "Jewish" of NT writings. See Luke Timothy Johnson's *Hebrews: A Commentary* for a fine resource for both preaching and teaching.

Let it suffice for today to mention the very beginning words of Hebrews as a kind of oblique entrée onto today's other readings which also include the rich psalmody drawn from Psalm 8 which offers an important insight into what we might call "theological anthropology," humanity looked at in the light of God's living Word. Here Hebrews offers this insight into God's Word by beginning "*Long ago God spoke to our ancestors in many and various ways by the prophets, but in these last days God has spoken to us by a son, whom God appointed heir of all things, through whom God also created the worlds* (plural, notice!). *He is the reflection of God's glory and the exact imprint of God's very being, and sustains all things by his powerful word*" (1:1–3a). Here we're reminded that for us who claim the name "Christians." Jesus is God's ultimate Word, not God's only word, mind you, but the key to interpreting, to understanding, to communicating all that God has done and spoken from the first moment of creation until now—and on through eternity.

So let's test this out by turning to our Gospel reading from Mark 10 in which we find Jesus himself interpreting scripture, specifically a portion of Genesis 2, the so-called second creation account. I use the word "test" for this is just what the Pharisees have in mind by asking Jesus the question, "*Is it lawful for a man to divorce his wife?*" Jesus answers, as was his habit, by asking a question in return, "*What did Moses command you?*" which they promptly answer by saying, in effect, that Moses says a man can divorce his wife. But that's not the end of it, for Jesus goes on to say, "*Because of your hardness of heart he wrote this commandment for you,*" and then does a deft jump back over the Mosaic law to the second creation account in Genesis, the book of beginnings. Here he cites God's creation of man and woman, of the two becoming one flesh, and concludes his citation with God's declaration, "*Therefore what God has joined together, let no one separate.*" This is all he tells the Pharisees, notice, leaving it to up to them to answer their own question from the scriptures he cites. But with his disciples he shares a further insight which might sound to us like a clear "No" but in reality does not make his decision quite that black and white. "*Whoever divorces his wife and marries another commits adultery against her; and if she divorces her husband and marries another, she commits adultery*" (vv 2–12), he says, which is really raising the level of the breach to a breaking of the sixth commandment and not just an interpretation of a lesser law of Moses. Yet Jesus does not provide a simple "Yes" or "No" to the Pharisees' question in either a direct or comprehensive sense.

We usually take this to mean that Jesus' evidently is declaring his opposition to divorce of any kind, since it results in the sin of adultery, contrary to the Mosaic law which allowed divorce when initiated by the man with a variety of rationales argued by the rabbis. But Jesus here jumps right over the law to God's intentions in creation, perhaps as a way of avoiding the clearly patriarchal bias of the Mosaic law which, in effect, holds both husbands and wives to a higher standard rooted in God's creative Word in creation itself. This, essentially, is the position I understand the Roman Catholic Church strives to maintain while other churches, including my own ELCA, understand divorce as participating in the sinful brokenness of human beings and our relationships and can be therefore sometimes the lesser of evils. Jesus wants us to see that marriage (and I would argue similarly on behalf of same-sex marriage) is not just a matter of law, although it is at least that, but has its roots in our created humanity.

Further, I hear God's earlier Word in Genesis 2:18 as the even more determinative word about the nature of us as human beings, about our theological anthropology, if you will. And that Word is the definitive "Not good" we hear God utter after the astonishing series of "good"s that we hear in the first creation account culminating in the "very good" over the creation as it is culminated in the calling into being of the (undifferentiated) "human one" or "earthling." After all the "good"s God declares that it is "*not good that the man should be alone*" (v 18). I hear this as God's definitive declaration that to be human is to be in relationship, and as the intervening, humorous story of God creating the animals to see if they fit the human one's need for companionship shows, God intends to do something about it. We are not fully human without being in relationship with other humans is what the story suggests, and, of course, the sexual and gender complementarity of man and woman here becomes for us the prime example—over time heterosexual marriage becoming the institutional form this relationship takes. But I do not hear Genesis 2:18 nor Jesus' words on divorce as some kind of limiting, rule-making that constitutes a new "law." Jesus constitutionally wasn't into law-making but law-fulfilling, fulfilling the spirit of the law (as in his words about sabbath-keeping) rather than somehow "protecting" the law from law-breakers as the Pharisaic intention to erect a "hedge" about the law by multiplying "dos" and "don'ts" was in danger of doing.[26] "When Love is Found" (*With One Voice* #749) is a rare hymn appropriate to these texts although the oldie "What God Ordains is Good Indeed" (*ELW* #776) might work as well.

---

26. See here my essay "The Church and Same-Sex Relationships," 440–451 as well as Lehman's posthumously published *The Decalogue and a Human Future* 55–92.

Lectionary 28, Proper 23

Psalm 90:12–17
Amos 5:6–7, 10–15
Hebrews 4:12–16
Mark 10:17–31

So teach us to count our days that we may gain a wise heart.

—Psalm 90:12

The Needle's Eye

Next to the window in my old church study, where I couldn't help but see it every day, hung a framed cartoon from an old edition of the *National Lampoon* magazine. It's a spoof of a Medici rose window from the cathedral in Florence depicting a laughing camel leaping with ease through the eye of a needle. The superscription reads: "a recurring motif in works commissioned by the wealthier patrons of Renaissance religious art." The Latin inscription on the window itself reads, "*Dives Vincet*," or "Wealth Wins." It's, as I say, a spoof, but a well done one, and so it was always fun to watch the faces of visitors to my office to see whether or how long it took them to "get it."

Just outside the street-side window next to where my grinning camel hung, most every day on the sidewalk would sit, or often recline, an old, deeply tanned, dirty and wrinkled woman who I assumed was homeless since she usually had with her a shopping cart full of belongings. She seemed oblivious to those walking by on the busy boulevard, even to the point of sometimes changing her clothes right there in the open, often chattering to herself and smoking. She never asked for anything, as other homeless folks in our neighborhood would, but seemed content to lean up against the other side of the wall on which my grinning camel hung, a scene, I sometimes thought, not so far removed from the streets of Calcutta.

Maybe you've noticed how it's almost always the rich and the poor who populate Jesus' stories and encounters. He doesn't seem much interested in the "middling" sort of people, which I suppose most of us think of ourselves as being. But I'm afraid our middle class sensibilities really won't let us off the hook for we know that by any global standard almost all of us are among the world's rich. And the nameless lady outside my window is a continual reminder that, yes, as Jesus promised, *"the poor you always have with you"*—and as he added and as we always need to remember, *"you can show kindness to them whenever you wish . . ."* (Mark 14:7). But, and it's a big "but," the poor don't exist simply as an opportunity for the wealthy to share their riches. Jesus and the prophets before him, as Amos reminds us in our first reading for today, had a very realistic and down-to-earth attitude about God's demand for public economic justice as well as a stern warning about the danger of riches—about living in a society where the gap between rich and poor was large and growing ever deeper, as in Jesus' day and our own.

It's worth revisiting the Letter of James we were hearing from last month where Jesus' own brother's (and I expect his own) sentiments about wealth were stated sharply in a passage that we didn't get to hear read. Perhaps the lectionary choosers judged it simply too hard for us to hear:

> *Come now you rich people, weep and wail for the miseries that are coming to you. Your riches have rotted, and your clothes are moth-eaten. Your gold and silver have rusted, and their rust will be evidence against you, and it will eat your flesh like fire. You have laid up treasure for the last days. Listen! The wages of the laborers who mowed your fields, which you kept back by fraud, cry out, and the cries of the harvesters have reached the ears of the Lord of hosts. You have lived on the earth in luxury and in pleasure; you have fattened your hearts on a day of slaughter . . .* (James 5:1–5).

What a rant! It's so radical it may leave us cold, as we say, paraphrasing the rich man who comes to Jesus in today's story seeking to know what he needed to do to inherit eternal life. "I've done no wrong, I've kept the ten commandments and kept my nose clean. I've defrauded no one, I'm not an oppressor, I pay above the minimum wage to the guy who mows my lawn. I don't want the poor to be poor."

That's why it's so interesting that the man who came to Jesus seeking salvation is portrayed as such a sympathetic figure. We don't have to think of him as a hypocrite when he frankly responds to Jesus' recital of the commandments by saying, *"I have kept all these since my youth."* (I expect that it's his own mention of his youth as well as his evident enthusiasm that leads us to think of the man as young, while the text never mentions his age.) The Gospel writer even goes so far as to say, "*and Jesus, looking at him, loved him . . .*" I don't know of anywhere else that that strong word "*agape*"—love— is used anywhere else of Jesus' response to a stranger. And because Jesus loved him, Jesus told him the truth—he told the rich man precisely what he needed to hear. That he should go and sell all he had and give the money to the poor, because his riches owned him, because they were a burden to him and stood as a stumbling block between him and the kingdom of God. When the man heard this, Mark says, "*he was shocked and went away grieving, for he had many possessions*" (vv 20–22). I'm reminded of the old movie *The Mission* in which the former conquistador played by Robert de Niro finds it necessary to cut the rope tying him to all of the heavy armor of his former life, which has become an impediment to him as he climbs the mountain to his new life as a Jesuit missionary to the local indigenous peoples he had formerly massacred.

As the rich man departed in shock and sorrow in being confronted with the truth about himself, Jesus recognizes this as a teaching moment for his thick-headed disciples who were "*perplexed*" by what they had witnessed. And so Jesus—as was his habit—decides to have a bit of fun with them in trying to deepen their understanding of "*how hard it is to enter the kingdom of God.*" I like to think a caravan may have been passing by, as he smiled and began to spin his absurd image of a camel jumping through the eye of a needle as being easier to imagine than a rich man entering the kingdom of God. This "*greatly astounded*" the disciples and as they started murmuring among themselves the obvious question, "*Then who can be saved?*", the trap snaps shut as Jesus announces the true glory and mystery of the gospel: "*For mortals it is impossible, but not for God; for God all things are possible*" (vv 23–27). Do you need any better example of what our reading from Hebrews is claiming in saying that "*the word of God is living and active, sharper than any two-edged sword . . .* " (v 12)? "Thy Strong Word" (*ELW* #511) is a fitting hymn for the day as is "Take My Life" (*ELW* #583) or G. K. Chesterton's "O God of Earth and Altar" (*LBW* # 428) with its chilling confessional line, "The walls of gold entomb us."

Year B

Lectionary 29, Proper 24

Psalm 91:9-6
Isaiah 53:4-12
Hebrews 5:1-10
Mark 10:35-45

*For the Lord will command his angels concerning
you to guard you in all your ways.
On their hands they will bear you up, so that you
will not dash your foot against a stone.*

—PSALM 91:11-12

Servant Leadership

Yet again today's Gospel reading gives us good reason to wonder how the early church had the audacity to include such unflattering stories about Jesus' original followers. This, for me, vouches for the authenticity of such a recollection. Moreover, the fact that, like our Gospel lection of some weeks ago, this is yet another story about Jesus' own disciples jockeying for power and position among themselves, seeking preferential treatment from Jesus, seems to indicate that status consciousness was a pressing issue among Jesus' followers, a recurring, chronic phenomenon not only among the original twelve but also among their latter-day successors who collected and edited these stories for the church of their day—and ours.

Even more chilling is that today's story follows so closely on the heels of yet another of Jesus' passion predictions that wasn't included in our assigned reading in which Jesus is found trying to prepare the twelve for what lay ahead. "*They were amazed,*" the text says, "*and those who followed were afraid*" (v 32). If Jesus had thought that warning them of his impending betrayal and death would allay their anxieties, he was mistaken. For James and John—the fisher-folk brothers whom Jesus had nicknamed "*boanerges*" or *"sons of thunder,"* perhaps signifying a special liking for the two with this term of endearment that may have had to do with their native enthusiasm—brazenly approach Jesus to ask him, "*Teacher, we want you to do for us whatever we ask of you.*" Now if that isn't couched in the idiom of little kids, I don't know what is, as many of us who are parents or grandparents or, for that matter, have good, honest memories of our own childhoods, can attest. You know the scene, with those rapt, pleading, pathetic eyes gazing up at you in absolute trust. But, like anyone who's been around the block once or twice, Jesus isn't sucker enough to say, "Sure, whatever you want!" Instead in good, ol' Jesus fashion he asks a simple question, "*So what is it . . . ?*"

And they blurt right out, "*We want to sit, one at your right hand and one at your left, in your glory.*" Pretty cheeky, wouldn't you say, of these rough fishermen to seek preference for themselves, to try and take advantage of what may have been Jesus' special affection for the two of them? But Jesus takes their request seriously—though I expect, inwardly amused at their temerity—as he begins by saying, "*You do not know what you're asking*"—when they thought they knew exactly what they were asking. And then he goes on to pose what must have seemed a strange question to them: "*Are you able to drink the cup that I drink, or be baptized with the baptism that I am baptized with?*" With unthinking excitement they reply together, "*We are able*" (vv 35–39). Knowing the outcome of Jesus' story, we're in a better position to answer Jesus' question than James and John were. We may smile a bit ruefully as we savor the irony of their naïve enthusiasm and optimism, remembering as we do, how these very two along with Peter will fall asleep in the Garden as Jesus prays his heart out, as today's reading from Hebrews so vividly puts it, "*offering up prayers and supplications with loud cries and tears, to the one who was able to save him from death . . .*" (v 7). We remember how Jesus prayed in Gethsemane, pleading with his Abba "*remove this cup from me*" but then concluding, "*yet not what I want but what you want*" (Mark 14:35).

We know, don't we, that James and John weren't able to drink the cup and be baptized into the bloody death of Jesus' crucifixion—they weren't close to being able. Yet notice Jesus' response to their full-of-themselves boast, "We're able!" Jesus says softly, "*The cup that I drink you will drink; and with the baptism with which I am baptized you will be baptized*" (v 39). In effect, Jesus is saying, "Yes, my thunder-boys, you're not able now but in ways beyond your own knowing and willing you will be made able." We hear this knowing as they couldn't the strong sacramental reality of God's eternal promises, sealed by Jesus' death and resurrection, which would make them and the others able beyond their wildest imagining, beyond their strongest resolve, beyond their best intentions or even strongest ambitions. "*But,*" Jesus concludes, "*to sit at my right hand or my left is not mine to grant; but it is for those for whom it has been prepared*" (v 40). In other words, preferences aren't my prerogative, they're not within my power to grant, they're out of my hands.

And this is where Jesus' private conversation with the thunder-boys turns public, as word leaks out to the ten what James and John have been up to. Now we have the makings of a community squabble on our hands—hurt feelings and power struggles and petty jealousies all start to surface in ways that every community of Christians will recognize. "So," the text says, "*Jesus called them* together" but he doesn't any more than with James and John berate the disciples for their jealousy and anger. Jesus sees the brewing conflict as an opportunity, a "teaching moment," we'd call it, when he's got everybody's attention, the emotional temperature is high and the disciples, for once, are going to remember what he's about to say. He begins, cannily enough, by saying, "*You know how it is among the Gentiles*"—"you know how "they" are—getting their minds off themselves for a moment. "*You know how their rulers*"—the word also means "leaders"—"*lord it over others and how their 'great ones' tyrannize them.*" "*But,*" Jesus continues, "*it is not so among you!*" No way can that be your way! "*But whoever wishes to be great among you must be your servant, and whoever wishes to be first among you must be slave of all. For the Son of Man came not to be served but to serve, and to give his life a ransom for many*" (vv 41–45).

The way of the "suffering servant" (of today's first reading), as Jesus' early followers came to identify his passion and death with that of the prophesy of Isaiah, the way of the cross, is not the way of the world and its style of leadership. God's way is that of underwhelming us from below, not "lording it over us" with power and violence and authority from above, slipping into our world in the guise of that most vulnerable of creatures, a human infant. The thunder-boys had it all wrong. Faith doesn't seek seats up front next to Jesus, but God in Christ Jesus has "condescended" to take a seat next to the likes of us. Servant leadership is the way of the gospel, and that indeed is good news! Good hymn choices for the day might include "O Master, Let Me Walk with You" (*ELW* #818) and "Lord, Whose Love in Humble Service" (*ELW* #712).

Postils for Preaching

Lectionary 30, Proper 25

Psalm 126
Jeremiah 31:7–9
Hebrews 7:23–28
Mark 10:46–52

May those who sow in tears reap with shouts of joy.
Those who go out weeping, bearing the seed for sowing,
shall come home with shouts of joy, carrying their sheaves.

—Psalm 126:5–6

Blind Bartimaeus

In November of 1841, about this time of year, the young New England poet with the imposing name Henry Wadsworth Longfellow wrote a friend: "I was reading this morning, just after breakfast, the tenth chapter of Mark, in Greek (then a language known by more than pastors and classicists), the last seven verses of which contain the story of blind Bartimaeus, and always seemed to me remarkable for their beauty. At once the whole scene presented itself to my mind in lively colors—the walls of Jericho, the cold wind through the gateway, the ragged, blind beggar, his shrill cry, the tumultuous crowd, the serene Christ, the miracle." Longfellow went on to note that all these scenes took form in the poem he then wrote, where, he says, "I have retained the striking Greek expressions of entreaty, comfort and healing," though, he was quick to add, "I am well aware that Greek was not spoken at Jericho . . . I think I shall add to the title, 'supposed to be written by a monk of the Middle Ages,' as it is in the legend style." As you read and imagine hearing (or, better, read it aloud) the short poem entitled "Blind Bartimaeus" pay close attention to the beautiful Greek phrase with which the poet concludes each verse, the first a word of entreaty, the second, a word of encouragement, and the third, a word of healing.

Blind Bartimaeus at the gates/Of Jericho in darkness waits;/

He hears the crowd;—he hears a breath/Say, "it is Christ of Nazareth!"/

and calls, in tones of agony,/*Iesou, eleeisou me!*

(which means "Jesus, have mercy on me").

The thronging multitudes increase;/Blind Bartimaeus, hold thy peace!/

But still, above the noisy crowd,/The beggar's cry is shrill and loud;/

Until they say, "He calleth thee!"/*Tharsei; egeipai, phonei se!*

(which means "Take heart, he calls thee").

Then saith the Christ, as silent stands/The crowd, "What wilt thou at my hands?"/

And he replies, "Oh, give me light!/Rabbi, restore the blind man's sight."/

And Jesus answers, "*Upage; E pistis sou sesoke se!*"

(which means, "Your faith has made you well.")

Ye that have eyes, yet cannot see,/In darkness and in misery,/

Recall those mighty Voices Three,/*Iesou, eleeisou me! Tharsei, egeipai upage! E pistis sou sesoke se!*[27]

Now before you all go running off seeking another source of inspiration for your sermon preparation, let me assure you that what may have struck you as a lesson in obscure, mid-nineteenth century poetry or, even worse, a Greek tutorial, can end up being the beginnings of a pretty good sermon. I hope that some caught the lilting poetry of those few Greek words from the tenth chapter of Mark that so captivated the young poet so many years ago, as he sat down to read his Greek testament after breakfast (this a Harvard Unitarian, if I remember rightly)! My hope is that these

---

27. Longfellow, *Complete Poetical Works*.

three Greek phrases that Longfellow found so striking that he (ingeniously) incorporated them into his poem might also help us to plumb the depths of this same passage, which falling on the Sunday we often celebrate as Reformation Sunday with a different set of texts, we seldom get to hear read and preached upon.

The first of Longfellow's Greek phrases translated as *"Jesus, have mercy on me!"* is, of course, the heart-rending cry we know liturgically as the *"Kyrie Eleison,"* though here it is shouted out into the dark void that stretched before the blind beggar sitting along the roadside. Somehow his super-sensitive ears had picked up the news that the procession passing before him was occasioned by the presence of a certain Jesus of Nazareth. It must have been a scream that issued from the blind man's mouth, for *"many sternly ordered him to be quiet"* which made him only cry out more loudly. Here was a chance he was not going to miss, Jesus' reputation for healing apparently having preceded him. Think of blind Bartimaeus in his dark desperation every time you sing *"Kyrie Eleison."*

And *"Jesus stood still and said, 'Call him here.'"* Oh how the blind beggar's heart must have been pounding as those about him, who had just been berating him, now informed him, in Longfellow's second phrase, *"Take heart, rise, he calls thee."* No careful picking his way through the crowd but *"throwing off his cloak, he sprang up and came to Jesus,"* following his ears to the source of the longed-for invitation. And to Jesus' question, *"What do you want me to do for you?"* the blind man didn't miss a beat: *"My teacher, let me see again."* And Jesus responds with Longfellow's third quoted phrase, *"Go; your faith has made you well."* And immediately, the text says, *"he regained his sight and followed him on the way"* (vv 47–52).

Faith? What faith? The faith that comes only as a gift from outside of ourselves as we cry out into the darkness *"Kyrie Eleison,"* like Israel of old in our reading from Jeremiah (v 7) and receive God's promised but utterly unmerited healing. Like blind Bartimaeus we receive the fulfillment of the promise given in Hebrews, for indeed *"he is able for all time to save those who approach God through him, since he always lives to make intercession for them"* (v 25). And, eyes now wide open, we follow.

Hymns today certainly must include at least one new singing of *"Kyrie Eleison,"* as, for example, the South African "Nkosi, Nkosi" (*ELW* #153), the Chinese "Kyrie" (*ELW* #158), the more traditionally well known Russian Orthodox "Kyrie" (*ELW* #155) or Franz Schubert's "Kyrie" from the *"Deutsche Messe"* (*ELW* #152). Marty Haugen's lovely "Healer of Our Every

Ill" (*ELW* #612) is another good choice. "Amazing Grace" (*ELW* #779) also, of course, works with its well-worn words, "'twas blind, but now I see."

Reformation Sunday
(See Year A)

All Saints Day

Psalm 24
Wisdom 3:1–9 or Isaiah 25:6–9
Revelation 21:1–6a
John 11:32–44

*They will receive blessing from the Lord,
and vindication from the God of their salvation.
Such is the company of those who seek him,
who seek the face of the God of Jacob.*

—Psalm 24:5–6

Requiem

November will always be for me the month of my father's dying—a slow, excruciating death from emphysema probably caused by too much inhaling over a life-time not only of tobacco smoke but dust and chaff and fertilizer, so that, in the end, he had to fight for every breath. To die of emphysema is a death of slow suffocation.

My dad, for the most part, endured it stoically, and was fortunate to be able to die in the farmhouse where he was born, assisted by my mom and sisters and the rest of the family as well as the good folks of home hospice. I especially remember the horrible dreams that he would have that would awaken him in the middle of the night. Whether induced by lack of oxygen or the medication he was taking, or just fear of the dark and impending death, I'm not sure. But I remember sitting with him one afternoon after a night interrupted by yet another apocalyptic nightmare that especially bothered him because it seemed to threaten us, his family. I finally summoned up the courage to ask him, "Dad, is something in particular bothering you that you have such dreams?" And I remember him sighing and barely whispering, "Oh, it's just the futility of it all." The futility of it all! I can't imagine my dad, whose father had died when he was nine, preventing him from finishing school, ever using the word "futility" in his life. I'd certainly never heard him use such a word, this taciturn, deeply faithful, Norwegian-American farmer, who always let his garrulous, better educated wife do most of the talking. To his preacher son, my dad's uttering in his dying days his feelings about "the futility of it all," was a shocking insight into what his dying must've felt like from the inside. It was a real-life immersion into the world-weary honesty of someone like the author of Ecclesiastes that just blew me away.

November is the season of death and dying, and All Saints Sunday is a day on which we, so to speak, welcome "sister death" into our communion of saints, as St. Francis of Assisi sang in his Canticle of the Sun. In northern climes, and even here on the central California coast, nature seems to be dying before our very eyes, as the leaves in the vineyards turn color and as the sun heads south. One of my favorite *New Yorker* cartoons pictures an older couple sitting serenely in their living room, the wife casually suggesting to her husband, "Let's drive up to New England and watch the leaves die." And then there's my second favorite of a nearly bare tree with just two leaves still clinging to the branches, one saying to the other something to the effect, "This time of year my goal in life is simply to hang on."

November is also the month of the church year's dying, and the texts we begin to hear today on All Saints Sunday on through Christ the King Sunday are mainly end-time readings, some of them "apocalyptic" texts that remind us that to be a Christian is to live courageously in the midst of a world that is passing away before our very eyes. It's to know that we are living in the end–times—however long that end may be in coming. And what's more, of course, we are living in hope through these end times, living by caring for the earth and loving our neighbors as our way of anticipating Jesus' promised return.[28]

---

28. See my "Wit to Relax in the Face of the End" in *Currents*, 115–121, which in its original form used the end of the year and early Advent texts as well as the Pulitzer Prize-winning play *W;T* to argue that this transition-time of the church year gives us annually through our appointed texts the wherewithal to honestly face the prospect of death, both individually and cosmically, with God-given hope.

Our first two readings both offer the promise of a time when God will "wipe away the tears from all faces" and "will swallow up death forever" (Isa 25:7b–8 and Rev 21:4), a day anticipated in Jesus' raising of his friend Lazarus from the dead, a death Jesus himself had wept over. But as both Isa elsewhere (65:17) and Rev (21:1, 5) report, a new heaven and a new earth are promised, not just the end of sorrow and death. "*See, I am making all things new*" is the good news that sustains us through these end times declared by the one who reassures us "*I am the Alpha and the Omega, the beginning and the end*" (Rev 21:5–6). It is in this context of end-time hope that we remember on this day those who have gone before us in the faith and especially those near and dear to us whose absence still painfully is felt and mourned. In a denial-of-death culture like our own that is at the same time so violent and death-dealing in so many creative ways, one of the most counter-cultural things we can do is to face the reality of our own mortality, of the fact that we too shall surely die, as we acknowledge honestly the death of our loved ones. We do so by proclaiming the most counter-cultural good news that it is possible to utter, that because of Jesus life has in death its beginning!

There are many hymns appropriate for today but don't forget the joyous "For All the Saints Who From Their Labors Rest" (*ELW* #422) which ought to be sung at more funerals as well as the contemporary rouser, "The Trumpets Sound, the Angels Sing" (*ELW* #531). I've long been a promoter of the little known, ancient funeral hymn set to music by no less than Luther himself, "Despair Not, O Heart, in thy Sorrow" (*SBH* #297).

Lectionary 31, Proper 26

Psalm 119:1–8
Deuteronomy 6:1–9
Hebrews 9:11–14
Mark 12:28–34

You have commanded your precepts to be kept diligently.
O that my ways may be steadfast in keeping your statutes!

—Psalm 119:4–5

A Commanding Love

A story I don't enjoy telling takes me back to a nice, candle-lit dinner my wife and I and our then six-year old son who usually was a good-eater and a joy to be around were sharing. But this particular evening Griff uncharacteristically began to make a scene, complaining about the food, making the meal a miserable occasion. Finally fed up with his unusual surliness I sentenced him to the solitary confinement of his room and dismissed him with these words of fatherly wisdom: "Griff you know sometimes we have to do things we don't want to do." To which he replied with the superior wisdom of a child: "But Dad, you never do what you don't want to do!"

Suddenly our dining room became for me a scene of revelation—the scales dropped from my eyes and I saw myself as my son saw me—I became King David to Griff's Nathan as he pronounced the prophetic judgment, "You are the man." And so like David, I too confessed to this prophet in kid's clothing, "Yes, Griff, you're right. I guess I don't very often do things I don't want to do, even though I know I should. I guess I'm basically pretty selfish."

Today's Gospel describes a scribe approaching Jesus, having heard him disputing with the Sadducees. Apparently admiring Jesus' answers, he asked Jesus the bottom-line, religious question, *"Which commandment is the first of all?"* This was actually a common if fundamental question which the rabbis of the day enjoyed discussing. And Jesus begins his answer by confessing the *shema* of his people, perhaps the equivalent of the Lord's Prayer which faithful Jews recited three times daily, which declared love of God with all one's being to be the foundation of the law. Jesus quotes the original almost exactly as found in today's Hebrew scripture reading from Deuteronomy 6: *"Hear, O Israel: the Lord our God, the Lord is one; you shall love the Lord your God with all your heart, and with all your soul, and with all your mind, and with all your strength"* (v 30). The only change is Jesus' addition of *"with all your mind"* to *"heart,"* *"soul"* and *"strength,"* make of this what you will. This is the first commandment, Jesus says, but as so often is the case he isn't content to merely answer a question. For immediately he goes on to quote another text from torah (Lev 19:18) which he says is *"the second"*: *"'You shall love your neighbor as yourself,'"* and then concludes, *"There is no other commandment greater than these"* (vv 29–30).

We've all heard lots of sermons about Jesus' genius in attaching the Leviticus text commanding neighbor-love to the great commandment to love God with all that's in us. But even more, we're fascinated with how Jesus, using Leviticus, sets the standard of love of neighbor at the bar of our love of self—"*love your neighbor as yourself.*" I remember years ago receiving from one particularly prominent televangelist (along with every other preacher in the country) a free copy of his most recent book proclaiming the gospel of self-esteem as the essential message of Christianity. You know how it goes: We can't love our neighbor unless we truly love ourselves which then goes on to lay out a particularly modern (pre-post-modern) "therapeutic" understanding of the Gospel which chiefly is meant to make us feel better about ourselves. I think Jesus intended something quite different. He did not, after all, tell the scribe that the first commandment was "love yourself" and then "feel good about who you are."

No, the "*as yourself*" comes almost as an afterthought, for Jesus (as Leviticus before him) well knew that love of self needs no commandment for it's the most naturally human thing about us children of Adam and Eve—the desire and drive to seek the welfare of ol' #1, that triune god before whom we all bow down and worship—Me, Myself and I. And yet, by including those two words, "as yourself," Jesus revolutionized the law of love by rooting it in our genuine humanity as well as authentic agapaic love of self rather than mere self-regard. As the German theologian Gunther Bornkamm once put it: "We are most skilled in the love of ourselves; whether in selfish passion or in cool reflection, whether prompted by blind instinct or by some ideal, we desire our own self. Knowing this, however, we know what we owe the other person—because we know what it means to love ourselves so very well."[29] Or as Soren Kierkegaard once wrote: "If we are to love our neighbor as ourselves, then this commandment opens, as with a master-key, the lock of our self-love and snatches it away from us. Should the commandment to love our neighbor be formulated in another way than by the expression 'as yourself' . . . the commandment could not master our self-love so effectively. This 'as thyself,' truly no wrestler could clasp his opponent more firmly or inextricably than this commandment clasps our egoism."[30]

All of which is to say that the genius of Jesus' answer to the inquiring scribe is precisely the conversion of our natural self-love to love of God and neighbor that God makes possible and accessible to us in Jesus. For the two great commandments are really not commandments at all in the old sense of God's demands but are certainly also something more than

---

29. Bornkamm, *Jesus of Nazareth*, 113.
30. Kierkegaard cited in Bornkamm, 113–114.

mere "suggestions." They are the sum and substance of the new covenant in which God promised in our Hebrew scripture text for Reformation Sunday from Jeremiah: *"I will put my law within them, and I will write it upon their hearts; and I will be their God, and they shall be my people"* (31:33). The new and great commandment will no longer need to be bound as a sign upon our hands or as emblems between our eyes or written upon our doorposts, as we hear in our reading from Deuteronomy (v 8). For they are inscribed on our hearts as that commanding love of God that has laid hold upon us in baptism, converting our native self-love into the vehicle of neighbor love.

The scribe of our text caught on to what Jesus was telling him and, to his credit, found it possible to approve of Jesus' answer, saying *"You are right, teacher."* Jesus' response was to commend the scribe for answering *"wisely,"* saying, *"You are not far from the kingdom of God,"* a welcoming response that nonetheless, Mark says, led to no one else daring to ask Jesus any more questions. For who could improve on Jesus' answer? And yet the scribe was only at the threshhold of the kingdom of God and not yet within it. For he lacked the one thing needful which we might see as that desperate hope for healing placed in Jesus we discovered in blind Bartimeus and that Jesus called faith, Jesus the one in whom love of God and love of neighbor were incarnate and would be fully and finally revealed only in his cross made revelatory by his resurrection from the dead. You can't do much better than the Wesleyan "Love Divine, All Loves Excelling" (*ELW* #631) but do try the Ghanian "Jesu, Jesu" (*ELW* #708) as well.

Lectionary 32, Proper 27

Psalm 146
1 Kings 17:8–16
Hebrews 9:24–28
Mark 12:38–44

The Lord lifts up those who are bowed down; the Lord loves the righteous. The Lord watches over the strangers; he upholds the orphan and the widow, but the way of the wicked he brings to ruin.

—Psalm 146:8b–9

Year B
Mite-y Giving

The two "widow stories" we hear in today's readings, separated though they may be by eight or nine centuries of Jewish story-telling and biblical history, are remarkably memorable snap-shots of two nameless women whose unstinting generosity and sacrificial hospitality have become legendary for us people of the Book. The fact that they are nameless women who are so remembered is, of course, itself significant. For it testifies with eloquent silence to the social fact that women were more or less anonymous in ancient near-eastern society, as indeed throughout much of history, east and west, north and south. And widows, by definition those bereft of a husband, were the nameless of the nameless. For a woman's status and security were almost entirely dependent upon men—first one's father, then one's husband—who in a very real sense owned the females within their household. Hence the ease with which a husband could divorce his wife, as we encountered a few weeks back in our readings, when we heard Jesus speaking such stern words about divorce that to our contemporary ears sounded so judgmental and legalistic in holding marriage partners—men as well as women—to a higher fidelity, of mutuality and gender equality, than the law of Moses, or later, Islamic sharia.

The point is that the two women of today's stories being widows—women left without husbands—were consigned to living at the margins of society. That's why both Hebrew scripture and the NT continually hold up the compassionate treatment of widows as the mark of a people intent on living by God's plumb-line of justice and mercy. Remember how a few weeks back in the Letter of James, what I think of as the most Jewish book in the New Testament, we heard this declaration: *"Religion that is pure and undefiled before God is this: to visit orphans and widows in their affliction and to keep unstained by the world"* (1:27). Widows and children are the prototypical "least of these" to whom Jesus so characteristically pointed his followers as those to whom both justice and compassion were to be shown, as in the Book of Ruth, another widow story that is an alternative reading for today.

In thinking about these two widow stories—of the gentile widow of Zaraphath in the region of Sidon who used her last bit of oil and meal to bake a loaf of bread for the prophet Elijah—and the widow whom Jesus glimpsed dropping her two copper coins into the temple offering, whom Jesus somehow knew was also giving her all—her *"whole life"* the text says—I wonder what adjective first comes to mind as you think about their behavior?

It's the old-fashioned word "foolhardy" that pops into my head, a word that my dictionary defines as "thoughtlessly bold" or "imprudently daring." Is it just another sexist stereotype for our patriarchal scriptures to have selected two nameless women for these roles—to act the fool? Particularly the richly detailed story from 1 Kings raises our eyebrows, doesn't it, as we learn that this gentile woman whom the Jewish prophet encounters in the midst of a time of drought and famine is gathering wood, as the text so pathetically and poignantly points out, so that she could prepare for her son and herself a final meal before dying together of starvation?

Into this heart-breaking scene strides this foreign holy man who peremptorily commands the widow "*bring me a little water . . . so that I may drink*" followed by "*bring me a morsel of bread . . .*" (vv 10–11). No preliminary courtesy, not even a "please," but just a rude command. But even more amazing than the prophet's imperiousness is that the nameless widow did as he commanded, even though she did take time to acquaint Elijah with her desperate situation. How could she have done it? Was it mere social convention, an act of ancient near-eastern hospitality taken to its absurd extreme? Or might it have been sheer resignation to her hopeless plight, her just going through the motions to hasten the certain death that awaited her and her son?

Or might there be a strange sense in which God's own Word—in the person of the prophet and his rudeness—had invaded, intruded upon, this woman's private misery, giving this hopeless, destitute, starving woman company—"companionship," which literally means "one with whom to share bread"—someone with whom to share literally her last crust before starving to death? We might well ask, which is the greater miracle, the wonder of the perpetually full jar of flour and flask of oil which Yahweh provided or the miracle of the foolhardy generosity of this widow willing to share her last meal with an intrusive stranger?

The tale of the widow in our Gospel reading is a much briefer, leaner story—really only a glimpse—into another anonymous widow's life. Jesus is sitting one day across from the temple offering box, probably observing those very same behaviors that a chapter earlier in Mark's Gospel had led him in anger to overturn the tables of the money-changers. But here he was observing not the money-making going on but the money-giving. He especially noticed, Mark tells us, how "*many rich people were putting in large sums."* When along came a poor widow who must've seemed out of place in this parade of conspicuously pious and well-dressed philanthropy. Observing her closely, he sees her approach the offering box and drop in two small, copper coins—the lowest denomination of coin, scholars tell us, worth one-sixty-fourth of a denarius, a denarius being a common laborer's daily living wage. Not much, in other words.

But for Jesus, perhaps noticing the smirks on his disciples' faces, this has the makings of another of his teaching moments and nodding at the woman he says to the disciples *"Truly I tell you, this poor widow has put in more than all those who are contributing to the treasury. For all of them have contributed out of their abundance; but she out of her poverty has put in everything she had to live on* (literally, in Greek, her whole *"bios"*, as in "biology")—her whole life (vv 43–44).

This, of course, has long been a favorite stewardship text for preaching—and for mighty good reason, since Jesus once again is making money the shorthand way of getting at our attitude toward the trusteeship, the care-taking, that God has called us to exercise over the things of this life entrusted into our care but not our keeping. But in recent years I've come more to focus on just what Jesus is getting at in pointing out how this poor but generous widow is giving from her very poverty and not from her abundance like all those about her. Find ways to ask your congregation to consider what it would mean for us to give not only generously but sacrificially not from our abundance but from some particular point of poverty within our own lives. There's hardly a better hymn than the oldie "We Give Thee But Thine Own" (*ELW* #686) but try too Fred Pratt Green's harvest/stewardship hymn "For the Fruit of All Creation" (*ELW* #679) with its ingenious triple-rhyme in verse 3 "For the wonders that astound us,/for the truths that still confound us,/most of all, that love has found us,/thanks be to God."

Postils for Preaching

Lectionary 33, Proper 28

Psalm 16
Daniel 12:1–3
Hebrews 10:11–14, [15–18] 19–25
Mark 13:1–8

*Protect me, O God, for in you I take refuge.
I say to the Lord, "You are my Lord; I have no good apart from you."*

—PSALM 16:1–2

Birth-Pangs

I can't help but think of our Gospel story on this penultimate Sunday of the church year as yet another in the long line of Jesus' disciples' "gee whiz" experiences that Mark, the Gospel writer, seems so to so delight in recounting. Today's reading continues immediately upon where we left off last week, Jesus having directed his disciples' attention to the poor widow dropping her last pennies into the temple treasury. "*As Jesus came out of the temple, one of his disciples said to him, 'Look Teacher, what large stones and what large buildings'*" (v 1). In Mark's telling of the Jesus story, this is the disciples' first visit to Jerusalem and its temple. These guys, remember, are country bumpkins from up north in Galilee, and we can forgive them for oohing and aahing like any tourists from the hinterlands over the beautiful buildings that Herod-the-not-so-great had completed on Mt. Zion where Solomon's temple had stood before the Babylonian conquest.

But Jesus, not so easily impressed by the mere appearance of things, throws cold water on the disciple's enthusiasm with the curt words, "*Do you see these buildings? Not one stone will be left here upon another; all will be thrown down*" (v 2). And indeed, Jesus' words would prove prophetic, for as Mark the Gospel writer well knew by the time he had written his account some forty years or so after Jesus' death and resurrection, the legions of the Roman general and eventual emperor Titus would utterly demolish

Herod's temple so that today only a piece of its supporting wall—which Jews today call "the wailing wall"—is left standing.

But that isn't quite the end of this "gee whiz" episode. For Jesus, Mark says, then led his inner circle of disciples down off the temple mount over to the Mount of Olives opposite the temple. And there Jesus is pictured sitting in reverie, musing on the "end times." Here, interestingly, he's not making a personal passion prediction of his own demise, as he's done before, but prophesies regarding the end of all times. I can't help but conflate this story with the similar scene from Matthew's Gospel where Jesus is pictured lamenting over the city, "*O Jerusalem, Jerusalem, the city that kills the prophets and stones those who are sent to it! How often have I desired to gather your children together as a hen gathers her brood under her wings, and you were not willing!*" (23:37). The disciples ask their Master what sign they are to expect, signaling the beginning of the end and then follows what scholars have called Mark's "little apocalypse" which fills the thirty-seven verses of chapter thirteen with Jesus' warnings and advice regarding what will happen. In fact, we began the church year on Advent 1 by hearing as our Gospel for the day the tail-end of this same chapter.[31] In today's reading Jesus warns of the dangers of false leaders coming in his name to claim their allegiance saying "*I am he!*", of wars and rumors of wars, as well as natural calamities such as earthquakes and famines. But he's careful to point out that all this must take place and yet *"the end is still to come"* (vv 5–8). This is not the end but only the entrée onto the end.

It's in the final words we hear from Jesus in today's lection, however, that all this doom and gloom gives way to the good news of the gospel as he announces that all this *"is but the beginning of the birth pangs"* (8b). Now there's an image for you, one that Jesus seemed quite fond of when speaking of the end times, as well as that other famous bachelor, the apostle Paul (see above, Lectionary 33, Year A). Some of us—and especially the mother types among us—know very well what "birth pangs" are all about. In her extended labor with our first-born my wife actually at one point asked me to shoot her, so excruciating was the pain—despite the Lamaze classes we had subjected ourselves too which I thought were painful enough! This is the image that transforms all of Jesus' apocalyptic rhetoric regarding the end times into a revelation of that God-given hope that is able to sustain the faithful through all times of trouble. For birth pangs are, of course, pains worth enduring for what they portend, for their long-awaited, patiently

---

31. See here Juel's *Master of Surprise* 77–88 referred to in last Advent 1's postil.

endured, hopeful outcome is birth—new life. And so it shall be with us, Jesus promises, as the end-time becomes ever more imminent, as the kingdom of God looms ever nearer. As our brief apocalyptic reading from Daniel promises, *"There will be a time of anguish,"* followed by the long awaited *"time* (when) *your people shall be delivered"* (vv 1–2), a quite nice coincidence of imagery that becomes a useful play on words, I've come to think, "anguish" and "delivered" and "birth pangs."

And so, the Letter to the Hebrews counsels us, *"Let us hold fast to the confession of our hope without wavering, for he who has promised is faithful"* (v 23). This is the essence of faith, to trust that God is faithful—and not place false trust in our own steadfastness. I love the following words which serve well as a kind of paranetic encouragement and blessing: *"And let us consider how to provoke one another to love and good deeds, not neglecting to meet together, as is the habit of some, but encouraging one another, and all the more as you see the Day approaching"* (v 25). Now that's an image worth remembering—"*provok(ing) one another to love and good deeds!*" "My Lord, What a Morning" (*ELW* #438) is an up-beat African American spiritual with an apocalyptic theme which presents a nice contrast in mood to the much more maudlin-sounding yet finally affirming Scandinavian hymn sung to a Finnish tune, "Lost in the Night" (*ELW* #243).

Christ the King, (Reign of Christ), Lectionary 34, Proper 29

Psalm 93
Daniel 7:9–10, 13–14
Revelation 1:4b–8
John 18:33–37

The Lord is king, he is robed in majesty; the Lord is robed, he is girded with strength.
He has established the world; it shall never be moved;
. . . you are from everlasting.

—Psalm 93:1, 2b

Year B

What is Truth?

On this new year's eve of the church year, amid the end-time signs all around us, amid the seeming dying of nature, it's comforting to hear, it's reassuring to be told, the good news for today—and everyday—"*I AM the Alpha and the Omega, who is and who was and who is to come, the Almighty.*" Like the voice booming out of the burning bush, so the great I AM, YHWH, the "I AM WHO I AM" and "I WILL BE WHO I WILL BE" God is revealed as the one who comprehends us and all of time, who knows us more deeply than we know ourselves, as Psalm 137 declares, and who furthermore promises the best for us as the one who knew us before we were in our mother's womb.

"*Pantocrator*" is the Greek word for "almighty," the "Ancient of Days" as an older translation of our text from Daniel had it, literally meaning "the all-ruler," "the omnipotent," "the all-powerful." This is what those iconic depictions of Christ the Sovereign came to be called in Byzantine art, those stylized, Christ-enthroned, gigantic frescos that dominate the domes of Orthodox churches. It's interesting, though more than a bit chilling, to realize that following the Emperor Constantine's making licit and then establishing of Christianity as the official religion of the empire in the early fourth century how Christ the pantocrator came to wear the same gold-embossed ceremonial clothing as the emperor, to sit on a jewel-studded throne like Caesar, and to take on the aura of a high and lofty potentate, replacing the homelier garb of the lowly good shepherd or lamb of the catacombs and other earlier Christian places of worship.

Doubtless, this appeared to many Christians at the time as a far preferable situation to when followers of the Way were persecuted and martyred by the political powers. But to become an imperial religion, the official religion of the ruling realm, with crosses embossed on the legionnaires' shields, meant that the church would find it difficult not to adorn itself with the powerful perquisites and preferences of empire, which included enforcing its own monopoly on religion. As I learned first-hand years ago on a post-Lutheran World Federation Assembly trip to China, after centuries of the church being the handmaiden of western imperialism and colonialism, it is very difficult for formerly imperialized and colonialized peoples to see Christianity as other than the religion of foreign empire, as the faith of the foreign oppressors.

This is the historical legacy we live with as Christians, even, strangely enough, as citizens of a land whose founding documents assert the freedom of religion from state control, and (as we too often fail to remember) the freedom of the state from religious control. "Christ the King" Sunday, to use the quaint, older term, coming as it does always on the final Sunday of the church year, stands as a reminder of what we're always in danger of forgetting, that God is Pantocrator, the All-Ruler. Which means Caesar isn't. As our appointed psalmody for today puts it: "*ever since the world began, your throne has been established; you are from everlasting*" (v 2), the result being, as we heard the psalmist urge us a couple of weeks ago, "*Put not your trust in princes*" (146:3).

Today our Gospel text transports us right back into the middle of Holy Week, into the thick of Jesus' passion story in which John the Evangelist pictures Jesus in the midst of a dialogue with Pontius Pilate, the emperor's man as appointed governor of occupied Judea. The encounter is a curious one, for while we know it to be an inquisition where life and death hang in the balance, the dialogue nonetheless has a peculiarly detached and almost philosophic character to it. It begins with Pilate summoning Jesus into his presence and then asking, "*Are you the king of the Jews?*"—a pretty straightforward question that the governor must have felt cut to the chase. And he, being a good politician, knew enough not to unnecessarily interpose himself amid a merely intramural religious squabble among contending Jewish religious sectaries. To which Jesus, rarely one to give a straight answer to someone else's questions, responds, "*Is this your own idea or have others suggested it to you?*" (vv 33–34).

"What?" Pilate retorts, to paraphrase a bit. "What?" more than a bit miffed at this cheeky Galilean daring to turn a question back on him: "*I am not a Jew, am I? Your own nation and the chief priests have handed you over to me. What have you done?*" It's a question, please notice, to which Jesus gives no direct answer, not even a quotation from his people's scriptures. This enigmatic carpenter's son from Galilee just leaves Pilate hanging there until finally deigning to reply with his own oblique claim, "*My kingdom is not from this world*," a strange use of the little two-letter Greek preposition, "*ek*" that used to be translated "of" but more literally means "from" or "out of"—as in "deriving from" or "arising out of." "*If my kingdom were from this world, my followers would be fighting to keep me from being handed over to the Judeans. But as it is, my kingdom is not from here*" (vv 35–36). Three times Jesus uses this peculiar turn of phrase with the preposition "*ek*." So we can forgive Pilate his confusion, for asking again for clarification, in effect saying, "Now let me get this straight . . . So you are a king?"—meaning, "so what kind of a king are you, anyway?"

To which Jesus responds with what I see as a smile finally lifting the corners of his mouth as he once again tries to instruct the emperor's man in God's political science: *"You say that I am a king,"* meaning, "King is your word, not mine. What I can tell you is this, *'For this I was born and for this I came into the world, to testify to the truth. Everyone who belongs to the truth listens to my voice.'"* It's an ok translation but one that obscures the Greek that yet again has Jesus oddly using that same preposition *"ek"* so that in keeping with his earlier use of the word, he is really saying *"everyone who is from the truth* (who originates from the truth) *listens to my voice"* (v 37).

For some unknown (to me at least!) reason, our text ends here. But this isn't the end of the encounter, for Pilate responds to Jesus with what I imagine as a shrug of his shoulders and mutters in exasperation the well-known, age-old question, *"What is truth?"* (v 38). And as John pictures the scene Pilate goes on to confess, *"I find no crime in him,"* and yet, politician to the last, the emperor's man ends up allowing Jesus to be scourged and mocked and crowned with a wreath of thorns and finally nailed to a rough-hewn cross above which he directs the words to be written, intended, I expect, to irritate Jesus' religious accusers: *"Jesus of Nazareth, King of the Jews"* (19:19). Of course, the ironic truth of Christ the King Sunday is that Jesus is not only king of the Jews, but as we sing in the old hymn "king of creation" as well! (*ELW* #438).

Day of Thanksgiving

Psalm 126
Joel 2:21–27
1 Timothy 2:1–7
Matthew 6:25–33

The Lord has done great things for us and we rejoiced . . .
May those who sow in tears reap with shouts of joy.
Those who go out weeping, bearing the seed for sowing,
shall come home with shouts of joy, carrying their sheaves.

—PSALM 126:3, 5–6

Don't Be Anxious

People may think me perverse but this text from Jesus' Sermon on the Mount is absolutely my favorite piece of scripture for wedding sermons, speaking, as it does, a word of liberation from the need to worry into what is all too often a supremely anxiety-ridden time of a couple's life. But in a much larger way it's a word that has the power to liberate all of us from our preoccupation with "securing" our life by amassing as many things as possible. And most importantly, on this national day of Thanksgiving, it opens the way to a true spirit of "eucharist"—of thanksgiving and gratitude to God—for providing us with all the necessary "things" of life.

In many of our communities Thanksgiving has become an occasion for truly interfaith worship, when scriptures and songs and prayer from our various religious traditions are shared together around the theme of how our various communities express thanks in its broadest spiritual dimension. Best, in my opinion, is when we don't merely search for commonalities but offer the richest and best and even most distinctive gifts that our traditions have handed on to us, as well, of course, as giving us a chance as religious communities coming together to do so in frank confrontation with the most pressing public issues we face, both locally and globally and yet to do so in a spirit of gratitude.

Today's text from Matthew 6 is a most fitting text in which to present a teaching of Jesus that is accessible to all and that is not exclusive to Christian believers in its truth or the presentation of its message. Jesus' reference to the flowers of the field and birds of the air as messengers of the good news that by the Creator's good will we humans too can thrive without anxiety about the things of life is both a great example of Jesus' imaginative preaching and its universality. I've sometimes used in an interfaith setting a sort of fairy tale inspired by this text written by the great if gloomy Danish lay theologian and philosopher of the nineteenth century, Soren Kierkegaard. Let me try to summarize and give you a taste of his tale.[32]

The central character is a talking wood pigeon (a bit like Kierkegaard's contemporary, Hans Christian Anderson's talking animal characters) who at the story's beginning is found conversing with a tame pigeon. The wood pigeon begins by telling the tame pigeon how "I let every day have its own troubles, and so I get through life." The tame pigeon, preening itself, begins to boast about how secure its future is with the rich

---

32. Kierkegaard, "Anxiety About Subsistence," 95–98.

farmer who supplies it with corn. This sets the wood pigeon to worrying about its own security and it begins to spend all its time frantically gathering in as much food as it can. "He did not suffer actual want, but he had an anticipation of want in the future. His peace had gone. He had discovered anxiety about the necessities of life," the narrator concludes. "His feathers lost their glint of color, his flight its lightness. He was joyous no more; indeed, he was almost envious of the rich pigeons. He found his food each day, and yet he was not satisfied. Until finally he settled on the stratagem of flying into the pigeon loft with the tame pigeons where the farmer found it among his tame pigeons and killed it, releasing it of all its worries about the necessities of life."[33]

It's a chilling fable Kierkegaard tells, a sad tale without a happy ending. And it's doubly sad insofar as it is a retelling of our stories as well. As the narrator observes so tellingly, it's not our actual want so much as our anticipation of want which is for us the problem, to the point that our politicians can only appeal to our so-called middle class anxieties about taxes and entitlements and dare not even mention the real-life material needs of the growing numbers of the actually poor among us. Like the wood pigeon of Kierkegaard's story we're so confused and confounded by our anxieties that we've come to identify our desires and appetites with our actual needs. It's a story, of course, that sounds more than a bit familiar to Christian ears for Jesus tells his own version of it in his parable of the rich farmer, though with the wrinkle that thinking he has succeeded in "securing" his future, the farmer kicks back and takes it easy, luxuriating in his guaranteed future free of worry. Of course, he dies and Jesus' punch-line is a chilling one as he observes, "*a person's life does not consist in the abundance of one's possessions*" (Luke 12:15). Furthermore, Jesus concludes of the rich farmer, like the prophets before him, "*so it is with those who lay up treasures for themselves and are not rich toward God*" (Luke 12:21).

Being "rich toward God" begins with knowing whom to thank for the good things of life, as our religious traditions teach. The point isn't that we become indolent, spoiled children of an over-indulgent God. We are to provide for ourselves and our loved ones as we're able. And, what's more, we are to share our goods as well as our care and compassion with those in genuine need. True thanksgiving includes personal giving back and sharing as well as public advocacy. Being "generous toward God" is a matter of letting go of our anxiety and letting our gratitude overflow into

---

33. Ibid., 95–96.

everyday acts of thanksgiving. If anyone asks you how you know this, you just tell them that a little Danish bird told you. In addition to the oldies but goodies, like "Come, Ye Thankful People, Come," (*ELW* #693) try the more contemporary "Praise and Thanksgiving" (*ELW* #689) sung to a lively and well known Gaelic tune.

Bibliography

Anderson, H. George et. al. eds. *The One Mediator, the Saints, and Mary: Lutherans and Catholics in Dialogue VIII*. Minneapolis: Augsburg, 1992.
Bloom, Harold. *The Book of J*. New York: Vintage, 1990.
Bonhoeffer, Dietrich. *Creation and Fall*. New York: Macmillan, 1971.
———. *Letters and Papers from Prison*. New York: Macmillan, 1967.
Bornkamm, Gunther. *Jesus of Nazareth*. New York: Harper, 1960.
Braxton, Brad R. *Preaching Paul*. Nashville: Abingdon, 2004.
Brossend, William F. *James and Jude*. Cambridge: Cambridge University Press, 2004.
Brown, Raymond E. *The Community of the Beloved Disciple: The Life, Loves, and Hates of an Individual Church in New Testament Times*. New York: Paulist, 1979.
———. *The Gospel and Epistles of John: A Concise Commentary*. Collegeville, Minnesota: Liturgical Press, 1988.
——— et. al. eds. *Mary in the New Testament: A Collaborative Assessment by Protestant and Roman Catholic Scholars*. Philadelphia: Fortress, 1978.
Brueggemann, Walter. *Genesis*. Atlanta: John Knox, 1982.
———. *The Message of the Psalms*. Minneapolis: Augsburg, 1984.
———. *The Threat of Life: Sermons on Pain, Power and Weakness*, edited by Charles L. Campbell. Minneapolis: Fortress, 1996.
Bullard, Roger A. *Messiah: The Gospel According to Handel's Oratorio*. Grand Rapids: Eerdmans, 1993.
Cain, Susan. *Quiet: The Power of Introverts in a World That Can't Stop Talking*. New York: Crown Publishers, 2012.
Childs, Brevard. *Biblical Theology of the Old and New Testaments*. Minneapolis: Fortress, 1993.
Coffin, William Sloane. *Credo*. Louisville: Westminster John Knox, 2004.
Davidson, Robert. *Jeremiah and Lamentations*. Vols 1 and II. Philadelphia: Westminster, 1985,
Dinesen, Isaak. "Babette's Feast." *Anecdotes of Destiny and Ehrengard*, 21-68. New York: Vintage Books, 1985.
Edwards, Tilden. *Sabbath Time*. Nashville: Upper Room, 1992.
"Epistle to Diognetes." *Readings in Church History*, Vol. 1, edited by Colman J. Barry, OSB, 37-43. Westminster, MD: Newman, 1966.

Bibliography

Ericson, Jon Meyer. *The Rhetoric of the Pulpit: A Preacher's Guide to Effective Sermons.* Eugene, OR: Wipf and Stock, 2016.

Erlander, Daniel. *Manna and Mercy: A Brief History of God's Unfolding Promise to Mend the Entire Universe.* Mercer Island, WA: Order of Saints Martin and Teresa, 1992.

Evangelical Lutheran Worship. Minneapolis: Augsburg Fortress, 2006.

Fiorenza, Elisabeth Schussler. *In Memory of Her: A Feminist Theological Reconstruction of Christian Origins.* New York: Crossroad, 1985.

Forde, Gerhard O. *On Being a Theologian of the Cross: Reflections on Luther's Heidelberg Disputation, 1518.* Grand Rapids: Eerdmans, 1988.

Frost, Robert. "Mending Wall" in *American Verse from Colonial Days to the Present,* edited by Oscar Williams, 200-201. New York: Washington Square Press, 1955.

Gunton, Colin. *The Actuality of Atonement: A Study of Metaphor, Rationality and the Christian Tradition.* London: T and T Clark, 1988.

Hall, Douglas John. *The Cross in Our Context: Jesus and the Suffering World.* Minneapolis: Fortress, 2003.

Harrison, R.K. *Jeremiah and Lamentations.* London: Tyndale Press, 1973.

Haugen, Marty. *Holden Evening Prayer,* Chicago: GIA, 1986.

Heschel, Abraham. *The Prophets: An Introduction.* Vol I. New York: Harper and Row, 1962.

———. *The Sabbath: Its Meaning for Modern Man.* New York: Farar, Straus, and Giroux, 1951.

Johnson, Timothy Luke. *Hebrews: A Commentary.* Louisville: Westminster John Knox Press, 2006.

Josephus, Flavius. *Antiquities of the Jews. The Life and Works of Flavius Josephus.* Translated by William Whiston. Philadelphia: John C. Winston Co., nd.

Juel, Donald H. *Mark: Augsburg Commentary on the New Testament.* Minneapolis: Augsburg, 1990.

———. *A Master of Surprise: Mark Interpreted.* Minneapolis: Fortress, 1994.

Kierkegaard, Soren. "Anxiety About Subsistence," T.H. Croxall trans. and ed., *Meditations From Kierkegaard,* 95-98. Philadelphia: Westminster, 1955.

Lathrop, Gordon. *New Proclamation, Year B, 2000.* Minneapolis: Augsburg Fortress, 2000.

Lehman, Paul L. *The Decalogue and a Human Future: The Meaning of the Commandments for Making and Keeping Human Life Human.* Grand Rapids, Eerdmans, 1995.

Levenson, Jon D. *The Death and Resurrection of the Beloved Son: the Transformation of Child Sacrifice in Judaism and Christianity.* New Haven: Yale University Press, 1993.

Longfellow, Henry Wadsworth. "Blind Bartimeus" in *Complete Poetical Works.* Boston: Houghton, Mifflin, 1893.

Lewis, C. S. *Beyond Personality.* New York: Macmillan, 1945.

Luther, Martin. "The Magnificat" translated by A.T.W. Steinhaeuser. *Luther's Works,* Vol. 21, 294-358. St. Louis: Concordia Publishing House, 1956.

———.*The Martin Luther Christmas Book.* Edited by Roland Bainton. Philadelphia: Fortress Press, 1948.

Lutheran Book of Worship. Minneapolis: Augsburg Publishing House, 1978.

Meilander, Gilbert. *Friendship:A Study in Theological Ethics.* Notre Dame, Indiana: Notre Dame University Press, 1981.

Mendenhall, George. "Law and Covenant in the Ancient Near East," *Biblical Archaaeologist,* 17, (1954), 50-76.

Moberly, R. W. L. *The Bible, Theology, and Faith: A Study of Abraham and Jesus.* Cambridge: Cambridge University Press, 2000.

Bibliography

Montague, George M. S.M. "What Do You Do When a Promise is Broken?" in *Meet the Prophets*, cd, 1967.

Noels: A Collection of Christmas Carols. Edited by Marx and Anne Oberndorfer. Chicago: FitzSimons, 1932.

The Oxford Book of Carols. Edited by Percy Darmer, R. Vaughan Williams and Martin Shaw. London: Oxford University Press, 1964.

Pelikan, Jaroslav. *Acts: Brazos Theological Commentary on the Bible*. Grand Rapids: Brazos, 2005.

——— et. al. *Mary: Images of the Mother of Jesus in Jewish and Christian Perspectives*. Philadelphia: Fortress, 1986.

Postema, Donald. *Catch Your Breath: God's Invitation to Sabbath Rest*. Grand Rapids: CRC Publications, 1997.

Price, Reynolds. *A Whole New Life: An Illness and a Healing*. New York: Scribner, 1982.

Renewing Worship Songbook. Minneapolis: Augsburg Fortress, 2003.

The Revised Common Lectionary. Nashville: Abingdon, 1992.

Rhoads, David. *The Challenge of Diversity: the Witness of Paul and the Gospels*. Minneapolis: Fortress Press, 1996.

Rollefson, John. "The Church and Same-Sex Relationships: A Case Study in Hermeneutical Ecology." *Currents in Theology and Mission*, Vol. 29, No. 6 (December 2002) 440-451.

———."Invoking in Public." *Perspectives: A Journal of Reformed Thought*, Vol. 21, No. 8, (October 2006) 12-14

———. "The Wit to Relax in the Face of the End." *Currents in Theology and Mission*, Vol. 29, No. 2 (April 2002) 115-121.

Service Book and Hymnal. Minneapolis: Augsburg Publishing House, 1958.

Terrien, Samuel. *The Elusive Presence: The Heart of Biblical Theology*. San Francisco: Harper and Row, 1983.

———. *Till the Heart Sings: A Biblical Theology of Manhood and Womanhood*. Philadelphia: Fortress Press, 1985.

Thurston, Bonnie Bowman. *The Widows: A Women's Ministry in the Early Church*. Minneapolis: Fortress, 1989.

White, Ronald J. *Lincoln's Greatest Speech*. New York: Simon and Schuster, 2003.

Wilson, Richard. "The Parables" in *He Lived the Good Life*. Minneapolis: Willow, 1973.

With One Voice: A Lutheran Resource for Worship. Minneapolis: Augsburg Fortress, 1995.

Witherington, Ben. *Jesus, Paul and the End of the World: A Comparative Study in New Testament Eschatology*. Downers Grove, IL: InterVarsity Press, 1992.

Woiwode, Larry. *Acts*. San Francisco: HarperSanFrancisco, 1993.

www.ingramcontent.com/pod-product-compliance
Lightning Source LLC
Chambersburg PA
CBHW070917180426
43192CB00037B/1642